LUCINDA VARDEY

# BELONGING

A
BOOK
FOR THE
QUESTIONING
CATHOLIC
TODAY

LESTER
&ORPEN
DENNYS
PUBLISHERS

D0813230

Copyright © Lucidus, 1988

All rights reserved. No part of this publication may be reproduced in any manner whatsoever without written permission from the Publisher, except by a reviewer who wishes to quote brief passages for inclusion in a review.

Every reasonable effort has been made to trace ownership of copyright materials. Information enabling the Publisher to rectify any reference or credit in future printings will be welcomed.

FIRST EDITION

**Canadian Cataloguing in Publication Data**

Vardey, Lucinda
Belonging : a book for the questioning Catholic today

ISBN 0-88619-151-3

1. Church and social problems - Catholic Church.
I. Title.

HN37.C3V37  1988          261.8      C88-093105-1


Cover design by David Wyman

Printed and bound in Canada by Gagné Ltée
for

Lester & Orpen Dennys Limited
78 Sullivan Street
Toronto, Canada  M5T 1C1

This book is for Sarah,
for her spirit and friendship,
and
for my mother, Edwina, for her guidance.

I wish to thank all the many Catholics who kindly spent time talking with me and sharing their faith. To protect their privacy I cannot name them publicly, but they know who they are, and I am deeply grateful to them for their generosity.

Special thanks are also due to Heather Black, Giulio Brignani, Carolyn Brunton, Claire Crawford, Lee Davis Creal, Michael Creal, Sarah Krzeczunowicz, Alberto Manguel, Kim O'Brist, Linda Turchin, and Edwina Vardey for their constant help, support, and suggestions throughout the writing of this book.

My gratitude, too, to Malcolm Lester, for his belief, Gena Gorrell, for her clear thinking and her ever-watchful eye, and to Dean Cooke and Janice Bearg.

This book would never have been completed, however, without the care and meticulousness of my editor and friend, Louise Dennys. To her I owe my greatest appreciation, affection, and thanks.

L.V.

"The role of the Catholic humanist is to cultivate a more than ordinary reverence for the past, for tradition, while exploring every present development for what it reveals about man which the past has not revealed."

—*Marshall McLuhan*

"Surely it can be recognized that for many of us the understanding of religion is not simply a body of knowledge but a way of thinking, testing and searching."

—*A lay Catholic group in Surrey, England,*
*in a letter to their bishop*

"The Church will have to be further changed in order to remain itself."

—*Hans Küng*

# CONTENTS

# INTRODUCTION

I consider myself lucky that I was given encouragement when I was young to air my views, especially on religion and on Catholicism in particular. I had, like most Catholic children in the fifties and sixties, endured the many years of strict segregated convent education. I had been surrounded by nuns, the everyday clatter of rosary beads, the everyday chatter of prayers—"Our Fathers", "Hail Marys", "Glory Bes"—and suspicions were part of daily school life. I fainted regularly from the overpowering smell of incense at Benediction, or from too much fasting and abstinence before communion. I prayed and worked hard for indulgences and a shorter term in Purgatory (the place fairly close to the flame, but not quite in the fire), and was bombarded with the usual propaganda that goes with sinning and the saving of souls, the Catholic way. But luckily, where charity is supposed to start, clarity also emerged—at home.

I was born and raised in England, the eldest of a family of five children. My father was the only member of our household who was not Catholic. However, because my mother intended to keep the Catholic tradition—to a point—my father agreed to write hefty cheques to make sure our brains developed well in private grammar schools with names like St. Andrew's, and the

Ladies of Mary. He had married into Catholicism and, like it or not, he kept his vow.

His agnosticism was a welcome balance to the Catholic devoutness of my Irish maternal grandmother, who lived with us. To go into her room was like entering the grotto at Lourdes. I at one time found her on the floor in her nightgown with arms outstretched, and retreated quickly, suspecting I had tripped on something sexual. I was later told by my mother that this was the devout way to pray—flat on your stomach with your arms out on the floor.

My mother was really what can now be termed a "liberal" Catholic. I remember her saying once, "You know, if we lived in the time of Henry VIII and the Reformation we'd probably have left the Church." She in her elegant way, adoring large hats and bright colours, was at one time the only woman who sat on the bishop's pastoral council in the diocese. She was also a co-founder of the local Catholic *ad hoc* committee, which was affiliated with the National Renewal Movement. (This movement was formed by lay professionals in England in the 1960s, in protest to Church authority and as a platform from which they could put forward their views and concerns to the clergy.) My only memory of this is the intense discussions which could be heard regularly from the livingroom of our house around the time of Vatican II (the Second Vatican Council of 1962–65) and the publication of *Humanae Vitae* (Pope Paul VI's Encyclical Letter "Of Human Life", in 1968).

As a family, however, we were inclined towards mockery, and so there was nothing we enjoyed more than a slightly amnesiac priest giving a sermon, spitting his words and losing his place. We'd arrive back home to corner our father—who during the only solitary time he ever got, when we were all out of the house together on Sunday, was usually hard to find—so that we could re-enact the performance. My grandmother, who attended Mass daily, would scold my mother for allowing such a "charade", and after much argument my father would say wearily, "I don't know why you go to church at all, as you always come back in such bad moods." My grandmother would retreat to her grotto murmuring, "Jesus, Mary, and Joseph, forgive them, for they know not what they do."

But it seems, on looking back, that we were, perhaps through our mother's subtle coaching, developing the instincts necessary for Catholic survival—to be able to stand up for our own rights later in our lives, and to question where questions were due. This meant, predominantly, viewing members of the clergy as our equals, who were entitled to the ordinary reverence awarded others, but no more.

When I entered my early teens—a time when church attendance is usually replaced by more gratifying pursuits—my discovery of the opposite sex did not, surprisingly, distract me. There was another love in my life, and that was music. We were a musical family, and most of us could play the piano quite well. I had even advanced to the organ, through the aid of a humorous priest who introduced me to the basics of performance by showing me how to pull out the stops—"Just blast me, and them, out of the church as quickly as you can," he instructed. I loved the purity and simplicity of early sacred music, and at school had mastered the obscure theory of plainchant. The a cappella, the purity of the unaccompanied voices of monks—this was what religion and ceremony were all about for me. Playing the organ and singing in the choir were the reasons I got up early on a Sunday morning.

I realize now that I was no different from a number of my contemporaries. We all attended church in adolescence not because we were particularly partial to the Mass itself, but because of other commitments—to accompany the hymns, in my case, and for many others, mostly to keep their parents happy. Church attendance was a duty in our lives, like doing homework and helping around the house. The question "to go or not to go" only arose when we left the restrictions of home and school behind, spread our wings, and had the opportunity to make our own decisions.

I decided to emigrate. I landed a job in book publishing in Toronto and so left England and my family, at the age of twenty-one, for Canada, a country I did not know at all. I was a typical immigrant, arriving with two suitcases, a mothy old fur coat, and a yellow immigration slip. I rented a small room in a boarding house, and in an effort to get my bearings one of the first things I did was walk around the neighbourhood to locate the nearest Catholic church.

I had been led to believe, as a Catholic, that wherever I was in the world the old familiar "club" would always be just around the corner. At least, I thought, I would feel less foreign there, less of an outsider. So I headed off one wintry Sunday morning to a stark modern brick building swept clean of frivolity, flowers, and adornments of any kind. The only indication that this meeting hall was meant to resemble a church was the nasty mustard-coloured windows. It was here, after Mass, that I first experienced my Catholic crisis. There were no friendly, familiar hymns, in fact no organ in the church at all. I had naively looked to the priest for a welcome, had expected him to approach me and make me feel as if I belonged, but there was no feeling of community here, and no spirituality. I was hardly treated as a new member of the parish. Instead my money, what there was of it, was of greater interest to the priest than my presence.

After Mass, nobody stopped to talk to me on the steps outside; the cold wind blew as people hurried to their cars for home. I waited until someone inner-locked the doors behind me.

I returned to my room and wrote to my mother. What could I do? I had not been prepared for this and I was angry and dejected. I did not go to church again until a few weeks after I had received my mother's reply. She gave it in only one line, amid gossip about the family. "Don't worry," she wrote, "ignore the cloak:

4

it's what's inside that matters. Be bright and look for another church."

I knew, obviously, what my mother was saying to me—that I shouldn't give up on my religious association from one bad incident, or for that matter a series of unlucky ones. And I also knew that I had been jolted from a sort of smugness about the way I had been "practising" Catholicism. But where was I to go from here?

I was surrounded by friends and acquaintances who seemed content to call themselves "lapsed Catholics", who seemed to feel they had no choice in the matter. The old rules of Catholicism, beaten into them at school, suddenly had no relevance to their experience in society. For some, sexual expression was exciting and challenging; the last thing they wanted was to be reminded of its sinfulness and have to confess their desires and actions to some old, stale celibate, especially when their intentions were to carry on, not cease and repent. Others had grown bored with all religious activity. They had hated their time at Catholic school and had hardly been able to wait for the day when they could disown all affiliation. Yet others seized on their anger and disgust at the manipulative power they had felt from the clerical hierarchy as an excuse for religious rebellion. And some simply disliked the change from the old Latin Mass to the new, more spartan version, and felt that church attendance no longer nourished them. Was I now going to join their ranks?

I wasn't sure if turning my back on Catholicism was really the answer for me. Like it or not, I knew that as a baptized and educated Catholic I belonged to the Church in a peculiar sort of way. It was an emotional belonging—one that went beyond feeling like a member of a club. Yet as an immigrant in a new land, I began to realize that I could no longer operate according to the ways of the old country, where being Catholic had been so much a part of life. I had to say farewell to the old Church, the cosy parish up the road, the leading of romantic processions, the sprinkling of rose petals. I was forced to grow up in my religion, to enter a sort of adolescence of my faith.

But the transition was not easy. There were a number of choices I had to make, and there was a great deal of travelling I had to do before I could grow up spiritually to make those choices sensibly. The Church dilemma I experienced in my early twenties was just the beginning of the journey.

I had only my new-found friends, some Catholic, mostly lapsed, to talk about it with—and we did, endlessly. We all shared the problem. We were an angry bunch of people. We had no time for the Pope and his rules and regulations. They didn't fit with what we were doing: trying to live as Christians, occasionally going to Mass—avoiding communion because we knew we had "sinned" (mostly in a sexual way), avoiding confession because we considered it a farce. We were Catholics. We were riddled with guilt but we couldn't, as much as we tried, break free. We were, like it or not, tied to the pillars of the great Roman establishment.

Then, as we entered our thirties, a calming element seemed to descend upon our group. A few were relieved when they married, knowing that sexual activity could finally be condoned, but for most of us the questions went on—they just became, in our maturer years, more sophisticated and, in a way, more urgent.

We listened to arguments among Church hierarchy over the interpretation of the essence of the Catholic faith itself, the structure, the organization of the Church, and how it speaks to its eight hundred million members. We compared notes on parishes, different churches, which bishops in which archdioceses were politically right-wing and which more liberal. We didn't favour folk Masses. We searched for reasons for staying in the Church, and possible ways we could. We read regularly in the press about the dissent within the Church itself, about clergy dissatisfaction with the supreme authority of Rome (that at the present rate will result in half as many priests by the year 2000), about traditionalism versus liberalism and the possibility of a backlash to the ecumenical drive of Vatican II, as well as the growing power, in numbers alone, of Third World Catholicism. We argued about the decline in church attendance, in new seminarians, in Catholic schools; about the bank scandal, the celibacy issue, the sexism of the Church, the fight over contraception, abortion, and *in vitro* fertilization; about the drive for equality for women, and women's ordination; about the rights denied homosexuals, and the lack of compassion for those with AIDS; about the appalling standards of services in some churches due to the lack of intelligent clergy, and the growing disbelief in eternal punishment, and indeed in the very meaning of sin.

And we pondered the mess that we were all in.

We had nothing left of the old Catholicism of our youth; flawed it had been, certainly, but at least familiar. We had lost our conviction of exclusivity: we had become used to the idea of a more localized Catholicism, Mass in one's own language, recognition of other Christian denominations as sound and worthy of joint worship. But we had expected more informality with the clergy, more openness of dialogue.

Instead a dichotomy had emerged. Where liberalism had been promised, it was only half delivered. When the doors of Rome opened, it was onto a one-way street, as papal visits spread a hard-line message through the nations of the world. Yet the old messages of retribution for immorality, apt perhaps forty years ago, were alien to our own experiences and needs.

At the same time, however, bishops were taking stands on social injustice, delivering pastoral letters on the need for nuclear disarmament, equality in the work place, and caring for the poor.

So we slowly realized that, in many ways, we have neither one thing nor the other. Liberal Catholics, who feel the need to probe further, to question, to push for greater reform, are being ignored. The traditionalists, those who still fast on Fridays and revere saints' days and believe in papal infallibility, are also being ignored. Confusion—and even anguish—has been the result for many Catholics today. And many of the confused are turning away from the Church, in larger numbers than ever before. Yet the fundamental needs of Catholics on both sides are essentially the same: a sense of belonging, spiritual solace, ways and means to instil religious discipline and tradition into the lives of their children, and direction in educating their own consciences and coming to terms with their own religious beliefs, so that they can live their lives free of the destruction of guilt and doubt.

In many countries in the West—in the urban centres, at least—we can speak out freely about our concerns without fear of political or religious retribution. Considerable dissatisfaction is voiced nowadays by Westerners—thinking Catholics who question their affiliation with what they perceive as an out-of-date organization under a leader who ignores progressive discussion. According to a 1987 poll organized by *Time* magazine, 93 per cent of the Catholics in the United States felt it was possible to disagree with the Pope and still be a good Catholic. According to a poll conducted by the *New York Times*, also in 1987, 30 per cent of American Catholics are professional business people, 17 per cent of them earning salaries above $40,000. This is a powerful group for the Vatican to contend with. These people are, in many ways, the new Catholics; they have the education, the information, and the ability to attack the Vatican head on. They are used to speaking out.

There may well be millions of Catholics all over the world who have their own private religion, a religion which the Vatican does not want to acknowledge. But what about the enormous Catholic populations of some Third World countries? How can they confront the Vatican with the dilemmas of faith versus modern life? And what about the great number of people—in both the East and the West—who gain strength and fulfilment from the very dictates of dogma that are under attack? How are they to cope as the traditional certainties of their faith are eroded?

In short: where is all this discontent leading us?

There have been many books written about the Catholic Church and its policies, and the social aspects of its development and its diversity, but few about individual Catholic people today and their own beliefs. For me, the company of questioning Catholics is one which broadens my awareness and also introduces the possibilities of change within myself.

When I was contemplating this book, I spoke with Catholics of all ages and walks of life, men and women who opened my mind and shared their innermost faith with me for hours at their kitchen tables, the tape recorder whirling away and the coffee permanently brewing. I went back to my own past and background, to my mother's friends—those members of the *ad hoc* committee, now twenty-two years older and wiser, who still meet in each others' houses to share the Eucharist and spiritual concerns. The difference now is that they publish their thoughts and distribute them around the diocese. I began friendships with some priests, most studying or teaching at university, and realized that their concerns and problems were similar to mine. I walked in a garden in Venice with a gracious elderly contessa whose family had hereditary pews in the local church—now empty except for her. I sat in offices on hot summer nights in New York, in bars in Beverly Hills, in English livingrooms. I talked to Irish women, a homosexual priest, a Canadian schoolteacher, a Brazilian artist who had joined the right-wing society Opus Dei, a Scottish actress, an American businesswoman, a Jewish convert, an English mother, a journalist from Philadelphia, an Austrian businessman, a Polish woman lawyer living in the United States, and countless others.

And when I asked my questions—"What is Catholicism?" and "Who is Catholic?"—everyone had a different answer. I realized that there were no boundaries to the Catholic dilemma— it was one of the most heartening revelations to me, that men and women in so many different places were going through the same conflicts. Many were tired of the conflicts and wanted some light—relief and reconciliation. Others I spoke to were "lapsed", but after being away felt they wanted to return to be married or to baptize their children; or divorced Catholics who felt like lepers in the fold; or women who had procured abortions; or people who had lost a friend or relative to death and had begun thinking about their own mortality. And there were also those who simply wanted to deal with their spiritual needs, to develop a code beyond the loose Christian values.

Concerned Catholics face many complex issues when they question the perplexities of Catholic practice and try to reconcile these with their own consciences. Most people I talked to still called themselves Catholic, despite their doubts—Catholics can never ignore the faith, or the Church, or the fact that they are Catholic, even if they have lapsed or favoured agnosticism. Some of them found it impossible to associate openly with the Church, while others had, in their own way, found a happy medium. All of them recounted moments in their spiritual journeys.

Preparing this book has been a long and arduous task for me. I do not hold a degree in theology, and the only real study I did of the scriptures was at school. But the gathering together of material for this book—the people I met, the thoughts and concerns we exchanged, the prayers and questions I had—was, I believe, the best form of education. Through writing this I have defined my own path. I know there are parts of my religion I cannot accept, and parts I can live with.

For being Catholic is about doubting; doubt is very much a part of the questioning Catholic's life. There are doubts about one's personal, innermost faith—and these, for me, help to make it more stimulating. There are also doubts about the Church, for even if it is a formidable, authoritarian institution, it is also large enough to embrace a variety of opinions; this catholicism (with a small "c") has contributed substantially to the Church's survival through the centuries.

I believe that one has to define one's personal faith and then try to fit that definition into the institution, instead of trying to adopt a preconceived image of what the Church perceives as a good practising Catholic—or, alternately, leaving the Church altogether. The Church cannot offer this personal definition. It can only come from within the individual. What I have attempted to provide in this book is a look at the questions we face today, and the answers that some people have found on their own journeys, after much doubt and questioning. We will travel together through the eccentricities of Catholic childhood, the rebelliousness of the teens, and the early stages of adulthood, exploring the changes that occur. We will look at ways of dispelling old myths and hangups from the past, and focus on the difficulties that are evident in unifying personal belief with institutionalized religious practice. A new understanding of what "faith" and "Church" really mean can only emerge if we part ways with the old Catholic Church, and return to it today as equal partners.

I hope that my story, and the stories of those I talked with (sometimes presented here under pseudonyms, for obvious reasons), will help those who read this book in their search to define their own inner faith—and that they may also provide some overview of what it really means to be a Catholic today.

# 1

# THE CATHOLIC CHURCH

"The Church must remain Christian. Otherwise it is
simply not the Church of Jesus Christ, but just
another respectable club, association, coterie."

— HANS KÜNG

I recently came across a magazine article about immigrants to
North America who felt, for whatever reason, that there was
something missing for them in their new adoptive land. There
were a variety of examples given—removal from family, a thirst
for tradition, homesickness like the lingering dull gnaw of a
toothache. All of those interviewed had "made it" by themselves
in their professions and were successful by North American
standards, yet many were considering going back home. Some
actually did return to their native countries to pick up their old
way of life. But disillusionment set in, for they realized before
long that they were not the same people they had been when
they left. Nostalgia had overshadowed realism and they were
ill-equipped for the return.

I pondered this idea and wondered whether returning could
work if one went back like an immigrant, full of the same verve
and openness and excitement that accompanied the journey to the
new country. And then I wondered if the same approach might
apply to someone taking up the course of Catholic rediscovery.

I talked to a woman I had recently met, Nadia, an intelligent
blonde of thirty with her own law practice, a Polish immigrant to
America who, because of her imminent wedding to Bill, had to
confront her own Catholicism after an absence of fifteen years:

12

"I knew I had no choice but to return. I had had fun with lots of men in my life and my career was stimulating, and I never once felt guilty about having lapsed. But when I decided to marry, both Bill and I got to talking about our faith. He didn't mind so much about the traditional wedding and all that—but I did. I suddenly realized how important that was to me, and I found I wanted to go to Mass. How I surprised myself! Maybe the older we get, the more traditional we become. But you know, it wasn't easy—nothing is. I had hated my school days in the convent and had only associated bad, unhealthy experiences with my Catholic background. But when Bill started asking me about them, I found that many of them sounded stupid and irrational when I actually recounted them. And so, I suppose, I opened my own eyes. I knew that I had to tackle this paranoia head on so I started 'examining my conscience', a phrase that I never knew the true meaning of before. I began on the long road to change."

My own experience, of course, was a little different. I am a strong-willed and opinionated woman, and I was angered by the stupidity of many members of the clergy, but when I wanted to examine these feelings—and my thoughts about them—I hardly knew where to begin. Then one day, while I was sitting at my desk making lengthy lists of everything and everyone Catholic I could think of—which I believed would make a good start— I reached for Roget's Thesaurus to see what synonyms it could come up with for the word "Catholic".

I read, in part, "Broad-minded, universal, non-insular, ecumenical, liberal, free-thinking, patient, tolerant, long-suffering, even-handed, fair, unfanatical, enlightening. Galactic, planetary, world-wide, cosmopolitan, all-comprehending...."

Isn't this what Catholics would like to believe they are? Or it is, at least, what Catholics would like the Catholic Church to be. And yet the phrase "Catholic Church" seems to be a contradiction in terms. We refer regularly to "the Church" as the authority; we were taught as children that it was "true"—the "true Church". We sang about it in hymns.

One of the first people I asked an opinion of was a parish priest I knew and admired in England. I'll refer to him in this book as Father Jones. As we settled down by the fire in his presbytery, I asked his opinion about the meaning of "Catholic" and of "Church", and of "*the* Catholic Church".

He looked out over my head into the air, his rimmed glasses foggy and halfway down his nose, and made a steeple of his hands as he did when giving sermons in church. "You must understand," he said, "that Christ did not intend such a dogmatic Church. The organization Christ left behind Him was a very loose one. The only section in the Bible where Christ could be said to have founded anything was when He said to His apostles, 'I now call you friends, not servants.' One knows what a friend's wishes are and puts them into action. In other words He was saying, into your hands now, this is now your doing, you will have to take it from here."

However, there are others I've talked to who believe that what Christ did *in his life* formed the foundation of the Church as it is today. Through the special favours and instructions given to his Apostles, and by choosing a leader, Peter, to take his place as a figurehead when he departed from this world, he established the beginnings of the Apostolic See. He also clearly broke new ground by introducing specific guidelines for a Christian life, and thus a new religion. The Old Testament grew into the New Testament, to which the Catholic Church adheres. Christ also said that His kingdom was not of our world, and He declined to be crowned king in the traditional, acceptable way. Nevertheless, while teaching that faith and trust in God and each other were the essence of religious practice, He promoted the importance of adhering to rules, rules that made a good deal of sense, such as the Commandments—recognizable guidelines for living with dignity on a crowded and unorganized planet. Hans Küng, the liberal theologian, writes that for Christ

> the supreme norm is the will of God. His will be done!... But what is the will of God? It is not simply identical with a particular law, a dogma or a rule. From all that Jesus does and says it becomes clear that God's will is nothing other than the *well-being* of men.

Father Jones believed that too—and that the power of the institution came from elsewhere. "You know," he said, as he got up to stoke the fire, "it was due to the skills of Paul that any clear institution was founded. It was Paul who anchored the Catholic rock firmly at the core of the Roman Empire."

Paul's priority, after his startling conversion on the road to Damascus, seems to have been not only to clarify what Christ had said, by interpreting the Gospels in his own words, but also to lay down the law on acceptable moral practices for members of the early Church. These practices, though, seem to have been laid down primarily because of the need Paul had to establish good on-going relations with the civil rulers of the day. The opening passage from Romans 13 neatly illustrates how Paul managed to intermingle this message of civil obedience with his interpretation of the word of God:

> Let every person be subject to the governing author-ities. For there is no authority except from God, and those that exist have been instituted by God. There-fore he who resists the authorities resists what God has appointed, and those who resist will incur judgment. For rulers are not a terror to good conduct, but to bad. Would you have no fear of him who is in authority? Then do what is good, and you will receive his ap-proval, for he is God's servant for your good. But if

you do wrong, be afraid, for he does not bear the sword in vain; he is the servant of God to execute his wrath on the wrongdoer.

While we may well sympathize with Paul in his attempts to overcome the many obstacles he undoubtedly encountered while trying to set up an international organization, his emphasis on rules and regulations probably made it possible for Christians to interpret disobedience to his Church laws as wrongdoings against God.

In reading Paul's instructions, through his letters in the New Testament, to Timothy and Titus—who succeeded him as teachers and spread the word farther afield—one can recognize the origin of many of the Catholic Church's viewpoints today. For instance, of a practising congregation Paul wrote,

> Remind them to be submissive to rules and authorities, to be obedient, to be ready for any honest work, to speak evil of no one, to avoid quarrelling, to be gentle, and to show perfect courtesy toward all men.
>
> Titus 3:1

And about the role of women he asserted,

> Let a woman learn in silence with all submissiveness. I permit no woman to teach or to have authority over men; she is to keep silent.
>
> I Timothy 2:11–12

I asked Father Jones whether he agreed that the formation of the Catholic institutional Church began with Paul's laws as a code of practice.

"Well," he said, "it's true that these codes were instigated within the Roman Empire—that is, they defined the Church as a Roman church. The Roman Catholic Church."

Today the Roman Catholic Church is what Paul perhaps wished it to be—a huge international Christian organization whose authority in ethical policy and codes of religious practice is unsurpassed; a tight militancy with the Pope firmly entrenched as field marshal, the cardinals as generals, and the ordinary priests as regimental officers. Unquestionably a Roman Church still; but a Church oddly incongruous with the independence and non-conformity of Christ's way. "One of the troubles of the Roman Church," Father Jones added, "is that it operates with a boundary around it—that is how it was established. Whenever it has been threatened in any way—during the Reformation, for instance—it has imposed emergency measures on its people. Like a sort of martial law, in fact. This martial law, sadly, has never really been lifted."

I found Father Jones' comments on a Church with a boundary enlightening. But what about the other Church—the community of people, the greater Church?

Father Jones answered, "You know, people refer to 'the Church' meaning the Vatican, the Holy See, the archdiocese or parish, or another Catholic body commonly associated with religious authority. But there's also 'the Church' meaning a temple, a place of peace to escape to for prayer, thought, or solitude; it's a meeting place, a centre of the community, where sharing can be unifying and purposeful in a social way, beyond attendance at the services. But then there is a further extension of that Church to the home, office, or club, or wherever we find ourselves in a situation with other people—those we like and those we tolerate; this latter Church being possibly the closest to that with which Christ associated Himself. It's the universal Church."

As we chatted on about the meaning of Catholicism and the practice of Roman Catholicism, about the idea of boundary and no-boundary Church, I discovered that Father Jones was himself a convert to Catholicism. He had spent the Second World War as an Anglican minister. His broad liberal views were refreshing but not necessarily typical; he had come into the Church from the outside. Because of this, he showed little empathy when I mentioned the problems suffered by many Catholics educated according to pre–Vatican II tactics. But he was certainly right when he described the Church in terms of military discipline. Those of us who grew up within the Church were as regimented as any recruits—and the drill sergeants were everywhere.

# 2

# SCHOOL MILITANT

"In the war against sin, in the fight for the faith,
Dear Saint, may thy children resist unto death."

— "HAIL, GLORIOUS ST. PATRICK" (H.F. HEMY)

Some of the strongest memories of my childhood are the ones associated with church. The services themselves, with all the costumes and flowers, were like going to the theatre. There were the different smells of wood and incense and burning candles, the feel of the cool air, the cold touch of stone, sounds of echoing footsteps on flagstones, the colourful array of the stained glass, the glint of brass and gold and the dark crimson of Christ's dripping blood. There was a different language spoken, Latin, which added a musical touch to the proceedings. It was all so awesome and exciting. I had to be on my best behaviour for God. I was not to disturb others by talking too loudly, I was not to make the sign of the cross backwards, to stand when I should sit, kneel when I should stand.

Even though, since the dissipation of the Tridentine Mass (the ornate old Latin ceremony having given way to bare essentials), this Roman spectacle is rarely witnessed in local churches today, the components of Catholic religion and practice remain the same. They are the underlying specialities of Catholicism: the Sacraments, namely baptism, confession, communion, confirmation, the anointing of the sick, holy ordination, and marriage.

The purpose of the Sacraments is to supply a reliable intermediary between a Catholic person and God. This is the mainstay of Catholicism—"what the Church is for and what it is about", as the English journalist Gerald Priestland once wrote. But when we were young and in elementary Catholic schools it wasn't always clear that all the fasting and abstinence, prayer and clocking up of indulgences, were partly in preparation for the reception of the Sacraments of confession, communion and confirmation. And, for the Catholic child, this is where it all begins—since few of us, after all, can remember our baptisms.

Identifying the symbolic significance of the Sacraments is clearly an adult occupation, and neither the education system nor the Church was set up to be able to turn the complexities of rather advanced theory into a simple lesson for children. So the Catechism was introduced instead. In my time, in the fifties, when the strict form of Roman Catholicism was in its last throes—just before we entered the ecumenical times of the sixties and Vatican II—this Catechism was a sort of "highway code" to learning the Catholic faith.

It was easily written and easy to learn. The playful rhyming of the words sounded like verses of an old song: "Who made you?" "God made me," and so on. We were too young to understand the intent behind the question-and-answer formula. We were absorbing Church dogma in parrot fashion.

When I interviewed Father Wright, a tall, white-haired Jesuit who teaches theology, he expressed the view that the Catechism should never have been used in early education.

"The Catechism, to be fair to it, was written as a summary of the faith for older people. It was never intended by its authors as an introduction to things. When it was introduced to schools, it was first used by older age groups, and gradually it was dropped down the ladder to the younger children. And a great psychological mistake was made there, because if you look at the Gospels, the starting point is the love of God, how much God loves you. And the natural response is one of opening up, gratitude, praise, and saying prayer, and one goes from there.

The parody, the way the Catechism puts it, is—you want to go to heaven, do you? Right, if you want to go to heaven, you have to do A, B, and C; mind you, look at your X, Y, and Z too, as they will help you get there."

For us, learning the Catechism was like doing our homework in order to be ready for the test—to be spiritually prepared for receiving the Sacraments. And on the way, we learned too that we were really unworthy, that we were riddled with inherited original sin, being all Adam and Eve's direct descendants, and that we were viewed with disfavour by God. We, as young children, bore the stigmata of human failings like leaden albatrosses around our souls.

This remembered guilt was made clearer to me when I uncovered my rather battered childhood prayer book, *Jesus, Keep Me,* dated 1956 and inscribed "For dear Lucinda on your first Communion day". It is from my parents, but I see that the dedication is, much to my astonishment, in my father's hand. *A Prayer Book for the Catholic Girl: Instructions, Counsels, Prayers and Devotions*, written by a priest. Leafing through it I am stirred by nostalgia, by the musty smell of its pages and the crackling sound of its binding. I study the bits of coloured paper and holy pictures I have inserted between the pages, and a dried rose petal from some past Eucharistic procession falls into my lap. I notice the sad stringiness of the silk markers and the weathered look of the Mass section with its pre–Vatican II bilingual text:

> *Misereatur vestri omnipotens Deus, et dimissis peccatis vestris, perducat vos ad vitam aeternam.* May Almighty God have mercy upon you, forgive you your sins, and bring you to everlasting life.

It was the only missal I ever owned.

But looking more closely, I see now how opinionated, derogatory, sexist, and alarmist the text is. In the foreword, the young Catholic girl is told:

> There is *no more beautiful* object upon earth than the *soul* of a *young maiden.* To her natural candor and simplicity, God has joined the wonderful gifts of grace.
>
> She is clothed in her spotless robes of *baptismal innocence....* She is the *spouse* of *Christ*, without spot or stain, immaculate, undefiled....
>
> There is no *sadder sight* upon *earth* than the *soul* of a young girl that has turned aside from Jesus to *walk* in the *ways* of *sin.*
>
> My dear child, the loving Saviour desires nothing more than to keep thee. He has shed His blood plentifully to redeem thee. He lives for thee in the sacrament of His love. He is *ever present* in His Church to enlighten thee, to safeguard thee, *to keep thee.*

A well-intentioned message, perhaps, but not quite the way to a child's heart. Again, the wonderful imagery—the soul being a "beautiful object", she being in a state of grace like the Virgin Mary, without spots or stains (pre-pubescence being the desired physical and spiritual state), the word "immaculate" usually associated only with the Mother of God. ("Immaculate Mary, our hearts are on fire, *Ave, ave, ave Maria.*") And to top it off, it is made clear that Jesus was nailed painfully to the cross and died just because of *me* and *my* sins. A heavy load for a little body.

I go on to the section in my missal called "How the Knowledge of the Faith Is Obscured and Lost". There are tidbits of advice here, under subheadings.

By *Listening* to the *Voice* of the *World*: It is constantly whispering to you. It laughs at piety. It mocks at virtue.

It makes light of eternity. It lulls conscience to sleep.
It paints beautiful pictures of the pleasures to be found
in the ways of sin.

Farther down, on the subject of *Bad Companions*, is the
warning that they will "drag you down with them to the brink
of the abyss." And under *Reading Bad Books*, "There is *no more
treacherous* or *deadly poison*." (Television had not yet arrived in
every household in England.)

How would a seven-year-old decide which books in any
library were bad? Perhaps the ones that gave most pleasure, that
unfolded a new world for me: E. Nesbit's *The Railway Children*,
the illustrated *Heidi* by Johanna Spyri, and my most treasured
hardcover, Louisa May Alcott's *Little Women*. The censorship is
startling. Already there are fears about pleasurable feelings.

It seemed to us at the time that the Catholic child was
viewed, and rightly so, as an innocent loved by God and chosen.
But while we were given to believe, on the one hand, that we
were special, we were also told, virtually in the same breath,
that we were exposing ourselves to evil, daily committing the
unthinkable:

You will have such a horror of sin that your slightest
deliberate offense will grieve you and remain in your
memory. Your sin will *rise up* to *accuse* you.

No wonder my whole first confession period is lost in my
memory, blocked out by forgotten fears. But then and later I
must have referred to my missal, and contemplated its message
each time I examined my conscience before confession as I had
been instructed to do, trying hard to come up with variations on
my regular sins: "lying, disobedience, cheating, sneaking, and
forgetting to pray."

Father Jones, the English parish priest who converted from the Anglican faith, claimed that it was difficult to distinguish between so-called sin, and what might better be called the "teething pains" of growing up. Children of seven or eight, he said, were in most cases too young for introduction to the confessional.

"Often, in facing new situations, we fail to cope adequately, though we see with hindsight that we have been too casual, abrupt, rude, insensitive, etc. We need to learn and grow from such experiences, but being caught off balance is not in fact sinful, and a child can acquire an unnecessary load of guilt in thinking it is."

Elizabeth is a Scottish actress in her early forties, a redhead with lively green eyes. With her capacity to break into a number of different accents and characters, she is quick, funny, and entertaining; I warmed to her as soon as I met her, at a party in London.

I learned that she was pretty much alone in the world, having lost her parents; her sister and brother both lived abroad. But she was engaged to be married to a younger man, and she worked hard to stay regularly employed in the theatre, which she loved. She told me of her childhood in a strict Edinburgh convent.

"I used to go to the Stations of the Cross, and to say the rosary regularly, and I was profoundly influenced by the Redemptionist fathers; I used to go on retreats and do 'general confessions'—that was a week when a visiting priest would come, and if there was something you had done that you had never quite confessed to in the past—you knew your own priest too well, or something—here was your chance, with a total stranger offering you absolution. He would whitewash you. So I'd say, 'I am sorry, God, for all those sins I never confessed,' and then a great weight was lifted and it used to feel like a Friday night at home—clean pyjamas and clean sheets!"

"The child has no real understanding of sin as doing something incompatible with God's love," Father Jones pointed out. "Incompatible with their parents' wishes, perhaps, but right or wrong is then mere obedience or disobedience, being good or naughty."

When I was seven years old, I had difficulty, like many Catholic children, in believing I was a sinner. I wasn't a "good girl" or a "teacher's pet"—at school I was prone mostly to misbehaviour and rebelliousness—but I couldn't honestly believe that I had done grave harm to anyone, or to myself. I was more aware of the unacceptability to my parents of certain actions—which could probably count as sins by virtue of the fact that I can, on recalling them, feel twinges of guilt. These were such unsympathetic and uncharitable acts as not letting my young brother play in my games because he cried too much—which of course made him cry more; manipulating the new girl on the street into playing "baby" to my "mother", and then tying her into a pram for three hours and ignoring her wailing and shrieking; or, in a fit of jealousy, pinching my sister excessively, causing her to bruise. If these were sins, they weren't the ones I confessed, because I didn't understand the words "venial" or "mortal" and therefore couldn't differentiate.

I do remember, however, accompanying my mother and grandmother on the monthly visit to the confessional in a parish away from our own. I never questioned this detour, but looking back on it I recognize my mother's instincts for survival. She claimed that the times for confession in this church—"between three and four" on a Saturday afternoon—were more convenient; I suspect now that she preferred anonymity. The church was an older one which had survived the seizure of Cromwell's men during the Reformation. It was Norman in architecture, and cold and quiet inside. It smelled different, too—those years of lingering incense still in the air—and the holy water seemed holier because it lay in an ancient stone basin, not in a brass dish on a wooden stand. We would automatically drop our voices to a whisper as we entered through the heavy oak doors, and sometimes we were the only ones present. The confessional was not all that private, however, since the priest only sat behind a curtain; it was of heavy velvet and red in colour and seemed suitable for the occasion, but if you had a loud voice you had a ready-made audience in the pews behind you. My mother was all too aware of this and used to ask me to cover my ears, but when it came to her turn I strained them in my efforts to eavesdrop. (Is she confessing the swipe she took at me the other day?) She kept her voice to a whisper, though, and her confessions were always quick and slick. Granny took longer—she walked gracefully to the curtain, her head to one side, carrying a pained expression on her face, which would be transformed to one of blissful peace on her emergence. What *could* Granny have done? Minutes of whispering ensued. And then my turn. All my confessions were the same, as I rattled off the boring old list again. Sometimes I had to repeat my meagre sins two or even three times because the elderly priest could not decipher my mutterings; his hearing was bad and I, fearing exposure, would whisper right up against the metal grille, hoping that his ear, on the other side, was placed exactly opposite my mouth. I remember the bruise I would get from pushing my forehead up against the lower part of a very pronounced crucifix.

Bless me father, let's get through this lot as quickly as possible. The sun is shining, I want to get back to my game, so keep the penance short.

My mother and I would then roam the surrounding graveyard waiting for Granny to finish off her penance of the five mysteries of the rosary inside. What *had* she done?

If I had been interested enough, what variation on my list of sins could I have chosen? My 1956 prayer book had no problem coming up with a large choice, loosely based on the Ten Commandments. I whiz over the first eight and find that I probably could have committed quite a variety. Yes, I omitted my prayers; and my adviser informs me that "cor blimey"— a cockney expression we used at school as a replacement for "goodness gracious"—really means "God blind me", so I had probably taken the holy name of God in vain. "Have you yielded wilfully to thoughts, words, looks, actions, or desires contrary to purity?" Well, yes; somehow every time I sat in the school chapel I tried hard to decipher the sex of the cherubs on the ceiling. Was there anything peeping out behind that flimsy veil across their crotches? And wasn't Christ's cotton covering about to come down while he hung on the cross? "Have you indulged sloth, by remaining too long in bed?" Only when I didn't have to get up for school—yes.

Lyn, a novelist in her early thirties, was educated in a number of convent schools in different countries and recalls an incident when she was in India.

"We had a little garden—a vegetable garden—and each student was given a plot of land and we were all assigned different vegetables to grow. For some reason I was assigned radishes, and everybody's vegetables grew except mine. I was very upset about this and went to see the nun. Sister said that the reason the radishes weren't growing was that I must have done something to displease God. Now I was about seven years old, and I remember going through torment, searching my soul and trying to figure out what I could possibly have done wrong. I remember trying to pinpoint the exact sin and not being able to come up with anything. Of course, I subsequently found out that it's extremely hard to grow radishes in the type of soil in that area."

"I remember my first confession," the Scotswoman, Elizabeth, told me. "I was going to be the best little girl the town had ever seen. (No more sinning in my entire life.) The teacher said you must make a sacrifice. I didn't even know what a sacrifice meant. She said, you must give up something that you really,

really like. So as I listened for half an hour every night, and two hours on Saturday, to Dick Barton, special agent—a cops and robbers serial on BBC radio—I announced that I was not going to listen to it any more. The family thought I was mad and wanted to know why I was giving it up, claiming I would go crazy as I would just be gluing my ear to their door trying to hear it. I said I was doing it as a sacrifice in preparation for my first confession, and my father said that was very good, and he summarized the story for me every day so I knew what had been going on. This was the biggest sacrifice I could make. I couldn't think of anything else. It made a big impression on me. If you make a sacrifice like that, your soul will just be perfect."

We were immersed in images of black blots of "venial" sins lurking around our souls, which would be washed away magically as we left the confessional. Our young minds were full of the fear of temptation. We dreaded being like Lucifer, once the shining archangel, who fell from Heaven into Hell and never got out (Hell being like putting your hand in an open fire and keeping it there for ever). We began, understandably, to adopt feelings of guilt, weakness, and unworthiness, certain that we were heading in the same dismal direction "ever to be eaten with flames, gnawed by vermin, goaded with burning spikes", as James Joyce described it in *A Portrait of the Artist as a Young Man*. The idea of the existence of Purgatory, the weak alternative which offered salvation through penance, paled in comparison and was hard to comprehend. It was the image of burning angels and crawling serpents that was more intelligible to us.

As I turn the pages of my old missal, I come across the final word on "The Sacrament of Penance for the Young Catholic Girl", interpreted by our reactionary seer in the year 1956 AD.

The young girl should strive to understand and to appreciate that great *institution* of *mercy*, the *Sacrament* of *Penance*.

28

Were she to commit a crime against society, she would be mercilessly pursued across the face of the earth. Were she to be caught, she would be cast into prison, to wait until the time set for her trial. She would be dragged, without compassion, before the tribunal. She would be made to stand up so that mocking eyes might see. Her shame would be published to an unsympathizing world. The circumstances of her crime would be recounted in the public prints. Her ears would be insulted, perhaps, by the jeers, the angry threats of the crowd.

Witnesses would be summoned, and willing or unwilling, they would be forced publicly to testify. Finally, with the greatest solemnity, and with the utmost rigor, sentence would be pronounced upon her head.

*In this manner does human justice deal with human guilt.*

Let us turn now to the merciful institution of the Sacrament of Penance and let us see the manner in which human iniquities are dealt with by a merciful and loving God.

The sinner presents himself to be judged. He has committed not one but many crimes. His soul is stained perhaps with countless grievous sins. He has flung away his birthright. He has insulted and scorned and outraged his God.

He *draws near* to *Christ* and *sues for forgiveness*.

How *carefully* the *world* is *shut out*. No one hears save the minister who represents Christ. Everyone else is made to stand back. He is his own accuser; no one else is permitted to testify. He whispers his sins into the ear of the priest. He mentions the mitigating circumstances. He pours forth his sentiments of deep regret.

The *priest's lips are sealed*. In all the history of this divine institution, no priest has ever dared to break this seal.

The accusation is finished. The priest's hand is raised. *What sentence will be pronounced?* The only sentence that can ever be pronounced on a contrite and broken-hearted soul. "Go in peace"—in that sweet blessing of peace which thou didst lose when thy first step was taken in sin. "I absolve thee"—I loosen thee, I untie the bonds of sin that shackle thee and enslave thy spirit. "In the name of the Father"—that created thee—"In the name of the Son"—that died for thee—"In the name of the Holy Ghost"—that stands ready to sanctify thee, to save thee from the divine wrath and to prepare thee for an everlasting reward.

Perhaps the writer of this missal believed in love and human compassion. But the way he so badly interpreted the message of God's love to a child is possibly the greatest sin of all.

Such religious instruction, received by most Catholic children at that time, was inexpedient and inappropriate. It clearly established what was wrong in every child's life. And since we were feeling so unworthy of immediate communication with God, and didn't seem to comprehend that receiving absolution made any difference—as the priest kept reminding us by saying, "Repeat after me, 'Lord I am not worthy to receive you' "—the significance of our first holy communion was lost in a sea of bewilderment. Shortly after our first confession, we dressed up in white net, starched shirts, lace veils, and clean socks, and were led up the aisles as little brides and bridegrooms of the Church. We were full of the greatest fear and trembling, brought on not by the imminent reception of the body of Christ but by the fact that our tongues might not come out quickly enough to stop the host from dropping on the carpeted kneelers of the high altar or, worse still, on the priest's shoes.

A few years later, when we thought all the fuss was out of the way, we were introduced to confirmation, a sacrament which most of us couldn't really care about at all. But it was much more significant than we ever realized at the time.

Confirmation was the last attempt by the Church, through the schools, to indoctrinate its young members into the Catholic fold. In Canon Law it is described as such:

> The sacrament of confirmation confers a character. By it the baptised continue their path of christian initiation. They are enriched with the gift of the Holy Spirit, and are more closely linked to the Church. They are made strong and more firmly obliged by word and deed to witness to Christ and to spread and defend the faith.
>
> Can. 879

I can recall with clarity my own confirmation. We sang "Onward Christian Soldiers"—a most appropriate hymn for enlistment purposes.

> Onward, Christian Soldiers,
> Marching as to war,
> With the Cross of Jesus
> Going on before.
>
> Christ the Royal Master
> Leads against the foe;
> Forward into battle
> See, His banners go!...
>
> Like a mighty Army
> Moves the Church of God;

Brothers, we are treading
Where the Saints have trod;

We are not divided,
All one body we,
One in hope and doctrine,
One in charity.

Crowns and thrones may perish
Kingdoms rise and wane,
But the Church of Jesus
Constant will remain....

I remember being perturbed by all this; not liking the idea of the role of defender of my faith, and feeling very uncomfortable about the pervasive military image. I had difficulty in understanding the connection between the soldiering and the mandatory adoption of a saint's name, the only part of confirmation that consumed our interest. If you didn't like the name or names your parents had given you, here was your chance!

It was during preparation for confirmation that my thirst for knowledge of the saints and their lives took prominence. In deciding which one to adopt, I was forced to study who was up for grabs. I chose St. Anne—partly to please Granny (whose first name it was), but also because I liked the look of her in a painting by Cavazzola that I had seen in the National Gallery in London. Thus I entered my twelfth year as a confirmed Catholic, with my new name—Lucinda Mary Anne—to prove it.

At that age, just prior to puberty, it seemed to us that what we were striving for was purity and grace, in both mind and body. Boys were instructed to prepare for the life of the priesthood, and girls for the nun's habit.

I wanted to be Audrey Hepburn in *The Nun's Story*, or the Reverend Mother in *The Sound of Music*. Nuns were independent and powerful; they had their secrets and adventures—and besides, we noticed how good the food looked in their dining room compared to the fodder in the school canteen. They were obviously privileged. Not as much as the priest, who had the school children catering to him as well as the nuns; a priest was what you should really strive to be, it looked like a cushy life. But there were no openings for girls in that department.

So just when I was ready to enter a life of chastity, to throw away sin and temptation, just when I thought that I might, any day now, have a Visitation—not like Mary, of course, more like Bernadette (I would stop manipulating my sisters and turn to gaze on the Mother of God, ethereal and sparkling in the garden, or down by the millpond near the ducks where on a summer's day a lark would swoop and sing amid the grasses, and a great choir of angels would be heard; she would beckon and smile and then I would tell the world and join the Carmelites)—I began to become fascinated by the story of what Adam and Eve had done with the serpent.

# 3

# FORBIDDEN FRUIT

---

"For figs are not gathered from thorns, nor are
grapes picked from a bramble bush."

– LUKE 6:44

It was at the time of puberty, when my body was enduring
hormonal upheaval, that I experienced a sort of general confusion. This confusion was brought on not only by the pressure to
achieve and to make the right academic decisions about my future school subjects, but also from witnessing some very strange
behaviour by the teaching nuns.

First, in our school—when I was boarding—there were
mandatory breast development tests, which required girls to strip
to the waist and entitled a young nun to fondle their pubescent
bosoms. Then there was the odd nun whose duty it was to wake
me every morning. She did this by pulling back the sheets and
peeping up my night dress.

All my ideas of omnipotence, of purity and grace, vanished
into thin air, like the incense in the chapel.

Everything I did seemed to be sinful. Breaking school rules
was a sin, of course. We were accused of talking in the corridors,
whispering during prayers. It was sinful to gaze out of the
window during lessons to the gardens below, to stare at a nun
wandering around the bushes moving her lips to an invisible
rosary bead. It was sinful to be sick, or to need to visit the toilet
outside the regulated time or place. One new girl, who could not
hold on any longer, had no alternative but to urinate on the floor

of our classroom because the nun wouldn't let her out before the end of class. I witnessed another girl forced to eat her vomit one day, by the Reverend Mother herself. She had been sick on her lunch, and the rules were that lunches had to be eaten under all circumstances. The message was ringing more clearly by the minute: to be Catholic you had to strive to obey; there was no patience or compassion for human failings.

Now, if we had witnessed regular acts of saintliness from the clergy around us, we might have believed we really were unworthy; but instead, to many of those I interviewed for this book, a fair number of teachers in Catholic schools at the time— in the fifties—seemed bent on destroying the basic Christian qualities. To a child's eyes they preferred acts of cruelty and humiliation, executed "in the name of the Lord", over love and forgiveness.

One Catholic man told me, "In my high school, the assistant principal was a priest whose job was 'Prefect of Discipline'. He was a sadistic individual who thrilled in showing you his instrument, which he actually had tucked into his belt under his cassock, and any time he wanted to scare you, he would just push his cassock aside and show you this fierce piece of conveyor belt that he used as a strap. Literally—I once asked and he said that it was a conveyor belt cut in diagonal sections."

Some people made no bones about the fact that they were whipped so hard in their school days that there were times when they couldn't sit at their desks. Children fainted regularly during Mass because of the fasting they had to endure before receiving communion, and some were allergic to incense and frequently passed out or felt nauseated in church.

Being Roman Catholic was suddenly becoming torturous. There was not only the adherence to the order, with all the rules and discipline; there was now also the pain, discomfort, annoyance, and moral turmoil that accompanied it. Religious practice was of course obligatory. Religious knowledge, if you could call it that, was obligatory as a subject. And so religious anything became distasteful.

Joan, who was brought up in the countryside of southern England, is in her late forties now. She's married with two grown daughters, and works as a physiotherapist. She remembers not only incidents of her convent days, but also the tedium of being part of a staunch Roman Catholic family.

"My father was an Anglican clergyman who became a convert to the Catholic faith during the war. He became a very Catholic Catholic, with family rosary every night for years, to my excruciating embarrassment. When I was fifteen and having tennis parties and the like, when friends would be invited round, everything had to stop at 7:30, and the non-Catholics had to sit outside at the end of the garden while the Catholics were dragged inside to the mumble, mumble of the rosary. I tried to disassociate myself completely from it by thinking that that was just my father and he was eccentric, that was how I dealt with it."

It seems, from speaking to a number of Catholics who attended private convent schools, that what was lacking in their religious education was the spiritual preparation required for the very necessary formation of conscience.

The Church's new Code of Canon Law, published in 1983, states:

> Education must pay regard to the formation of the whole person, so that all may attain their eternal destiny and at the same time promote the common good of society. Children and young persons are therefore to be cared for in such a way that their physical, moral and intellectual talents may develop in a harmonious manner, so that they may attain a greater sense of responsibility and a right use of freedom, and be formed to take an active part in social life.
>
> Can. 795

Nowadays this is the intention, and there is no doubt that early Catholic education is far less rigid and cruel than in the past—as I shall demonstrate further on.

But many of those who had a convent education in the fifties were subjected to unrelenting pressure to stay in line. If they disobeyed, punishment was the response, rather than explanation, and as a result some became angry and frustrated. They were young adults defining their own needs, interests, and goals—a natural part of the maturing process. They were trying to incorporate these with religious practice, morality, and basic Christian values. A more flexible and sympathetic approach at school was essential.

There were other occasions when staff attitudes clashed with the students' idea of Christianity in quite a different fashion. John, now a tall, dark-haired journalist, attended an all-male Jesuit school in Montreal. He remembers an injustice that disturbed him.

"There were several incidents which happened together, but one of them I recall vividly. It was the incident with Antonio. His father was some bigwig in Italy who owned a large automobile factory, and who was very active in Italian politics and had to leave Italy for political reasons. He moved to Montreal, where he bought himself a thirty-eight-room shanty and shipped his kid off, with an awful lot of money, to the local Catholic school. The best one, of course, was run by the Jesuits, and it was the school I attended. There was a priest there I'll call Father Priest—for want of a better name. He was from a small town and had heavy homosexual leanings—he tended to grab certain pretty boys and make them feel the erection under his cassock. Father Priest was also a small-town bigot, so when he was confronted with Antonio his mind short-circuited. Antonio would come to school wearing expensive suits (he was only fifteen), and shirts made for him by the family's personal tailor. He wore gold stickpins through his collar, and had long collars about five years before America had heard of the long tip on the collar—which later became all the rage, but being Italian he was four or five years ahead of us. And of course he had weird glasses as well, with plastic lenses. He wouldn't take any lip from any priest either, but every time he passed Father Priest in the hall Father Priest would make some snarky comment about his manner of dress. Antonio didn't speak English very well but he could recognize the tone. He knew it was intended to cut.

"One day on the landing of the stairwell, Father Priest came out and made some nasty remark about the way he was dressed, and Antonio removed two of Father Priest's teeth—very efficiently. (Antonio had obviously learned how to grow up the hard way; he looked like a dandy but he was very quick with his fists.) Of course, the whole school said, 'That's it!', expecting the Pope to arrive in Montreal any minute where he'd take one look at Antonio and smite him to the ground until all there was left was holy dust.

"Whether Antonio was spoken to or not, I don't know. He wasn't suspended for even three days. It may be that the rector of the college was delighted somebody had put Father Priest down like that. However, that wasn't the point. The point was that he could get away with it, and the reason was that his parents gave an awful lot of money to the school.

"At the same time, though, the school was suspending a boy called Gerry Dwyer, later to become a superstar on a national hockey team, because he was found drinking a beer with his school jacket on. They suspended him from school for a week and suspended him from the hockey team for good."

The patterns of behaviour that the students observed were, far too often, less than edifying. But because no time was given to sophisticated, progressive religious instruction, the development of a more intellectual view of religion did not take place either. Some I interviewed told me they were given reading lists that included the French theologian Teilhard de Chardin and the

English writer C.S. Lewis, but this never happened in my school. We would have welcomed a lively discussion on the Old Testament as it related to the birth of Christ and to Catholicism today, instead of having to test our memories about the Acts of the Apostles. No doubt this exercise was to establish an understanding of the foundation of the Apostolic See, in which I, for one, had no interest at all.

Thus the inequality between pubescent students and their teachers widened. This is perhaps where the first damage was done, where the discontent that later grew into hatred of Church authority began.

It was a crucial time, a time when the Church and clergy could have reached out to children to make them feel welcome, to help them understand the unique history and cultural makeup of their religion, to give them support and encouragement as they grew towards religious maturity. But the process of this strict education did, in many cases, instil a strength of character, a belligerence, necessary for survival in the less-than-pure world outside. The irony was that the practice of Roman Catholicism wasn't much a part of it.

One 37-year-old New York publisher, Anna, who is also a competent marathon runner, was educated by Irish nuns in Pennsylvania. She told me, "I was miserable right from first grade. I stuck with it, but midway I decided that I just didn't want any part of it. The nuns had something to say about everything you did, no matter what it was. They got into the littlest areas of your private life. You had no privacy—you couldn't even dress by yourself—there was a rule for everything. I was an avid reader, though, and I read everything I could get my hands on because it let me know there was another world outside that bullshit. I read a lot of Jewish writers. I went the whole gamut, *Exodus* to *War and Peace*. I always felt an outsider to Catholicism—I couldn't understand reverence. I suppose, if I got anything out of it, it was from kneeling until my knees went numb from the pain, which has subsequently helped me a lot when running in marathons."

Many people agreed with me that the discipline, the rigidity of the rules of Catholic upbringing, help the strong survive, and prepare them for life in a harsh world. And perhaps there is merit in the argument that early discipline at school helps form a sturdy character. Germaine Greer, the brilliant writer and lecturer, was recently quoted in a magazine as saying, "If it had not been for the nuns, I probably would have gone to secretarial college and had streaks put in my hair and married a stockbroker. Certainly my family never intended that I should do anything else."

It seems to many convent-school leavers that nothing in the world shocked them when they left. Some spoke of the tameness of the outside; some missed the "Theatre of the Absurd" they had left behind. They can still entertain each other for hours talking about their crazy convent-school days. I find it hard to believe I endured those years of indoctrination. When I tell my stories, it is as if I am retelling tales from Dickens—or, more appropriately, Edgar Allan Poe. If so many of the men and women I interviewed had not undergone similar experiences, if I did not have witnesses, I might wonder at times whether those years at the convent were purely a fiction of my imagination. Even the place itself—that early Victorian, turreted, Dracula-like castle, with its winding drive and its groves and grottoes— is unrecognizable now. Where the playing fields and woods were sits an estate of twenty-odd new houses, and the chapel— with the cherubim and seraphim painted on the walls and dome ceiling—is now a classroom in a secular institution, the cherubs lost for ever under a sea of beige paint.

But at that time of our lives most of us had had enough. Religion and its restrictions were taking too tough a hold. We needed to break free, but to do so required adopting various strategies of rebellion.

# 4

# THE FIRST REBELLION

"For the gate is narrow and the way is hard, that
leads to life...."

– MATTHEW 7:14

We human beings tend to need to believe in something we
cannot apprehend or understand—something greater and bigger
than our meagre lives. Spirituality is part of our makeup. If
we do not feed it and let it live, unsatisfying substitutes can
emerge. Conflict occurs when we ignore the particular course
that is natural to us, or when we do not recognize the need that
so many of us have for spiritual nourishment in the journey
from childhood to adulthood. I don't think it is presumptuous
to say that a lot of Catholics who rebelled against their religious
education and background were fighting that transition. Many of
those I spoke to instantly recalled their rebellious acts.

We were then, in our last days of school, unprepared for
carrying our Catholic label into the outside world. We were,
in fact, mostly bored with religion. I remember witnessing this
boredom in my own brother, when the bishop came to our lowly
parish church. Giles, then sixteen, no longer fitted the role of
saintly altar boy, his vestments tight-fitting and short enough to
reveal his jeans and mismatched socks underneath. However,
being the eldest server, he was given the honour of carrying the
brass crucifix ahead of His Excellency in the procession, and was
responsible for it throughout the Mass. He fell asleep during the
Homily, awakening, as we all did, to the crash of splintering glass

as the crucifix destroyed the sacristy lamp. Granny was horrified. The rest of us were obviously amused.

In my final year at grammar school I was part of a class of thirty girls, whom I grouped into three categories—the Marys, the Elizabeths, and the Magdalens.

*The Marys* were the good types, who toed the line and would either become nuns or keep themselves—virginal and unsullied—for an early marriage.

*The Elizabeths* were the highly intelligent, heading-for-university know-alls, whose outstanding examination results made you wince. If they did not become teachers in Catholic schools, they would marry army generals, multiply fully, and still go to church. (I named them after the biblical Elizabeth who confirmed Mary's pregnancy—just out of the blue—at the Visitation.)

*The Magdalens* (the repentant whores)—of which I was one—had fun, were rebellious and innovative, and discovered sex early, mostly with the schoolboys nearby. (The head of our group was tall and blonde, and was voted leader because she managed not only to strip down to her underwear in the company of a boy, but also to actually "do it", earnestly, with the Head Boy of the school down the road.) The rest of us were dreamers rather than doers, but our activities were definitely more stimulating than the Acts of the Apostles.

The Magdalens' mission was to turn all subjects academic and religious to sex. Sister Bernadette in Biology was forced to teach reproduction, using the human body instead of a rabbit, and Sister Marie's famous red box (originally created for us to drop soul-searching questions about the New Testament into) was overflowing with queries of a more earthly nature, which she had to answer every Friday afternoon. The Magdalens joined forces one day to pressure her into answering what we announced to be a vital religious question, "Can any girl get pregnant *without* having sexual intercourse?" And she, trembling and pink, actually answered in the affirmative, which goaded us further. The poor nun was subjected to so much pressure to produce evidence that she ended up drawing a larger-than-life-size penis on the blackboard, close up against a mass of white chalk curls which were meant to resemble female pubic hair. "If you get this close, it is possible for sperm to escape," she said.

An obsession with sex is naturally all part of growing up, but for a young Catholic girl it had an added dimension in those days. For many girls, it represented rebellion against the purity and grace they had been taught was theirs, and a chance to be free to make a choice. For the women I talked to, this rebellion manifested itself predominantly in the loss of virginity, an act which itself affirmed a farewell to the oppression of their Catholic childhood.

The Scottish actress Elizabeth approached it in a purely clinical fashion. "One day I looked in the mirror and said to myself, 'You'd better do it or you'll go nuts.' I knew I was not going to get married for a long while and the thought of preserving my virginity seemed unnatural to me. I didn't feel guilty about it because I knew God knew I needed to lose it— He understood. And I wasn't promiscuous—I was too damned scared! At home, all talk of sex was repressed, so I knew nothing about birth control, sexual matters, or anything, but I went out and lost it as planned."

Tess is a medical doctor from Dublin—tall, thin, with a head of jet black hair. The eldest of six children, she remembers, "Despite the fact that I knew both my parents would be very hurt, and I knew you shouldn't sleep with anybody before you were married, and I knew I didn't want to sleep with anybody just so I wouldn't have to remain a virgin, suddenly I had to get rid of it. Just like that—cold-blooded I was about it. There was no religious trauma for me."

I was not as positive or clinical about losing my virginity as Elizabeth or Tess, since I had been in love with the boy next door for one year through the hedge, and had taken it further for the two after that in his parents' garage. Things were getting tense, and his Protestant patience was wearing thin. I became aware that there was no other choice than to go ahead and lose the precious affliction. The act done, I knew there was no turning back, and I was positive that I had not committed a sin. Why, I asked myself, had I even waited so long? This was not an act done expediently out of lust; it was an act of love and to avoid it now seemed to me to be living a sin.

I was, at the time, attempting to withdraw from the regularity of the tedious visits to the confessional, yet I now had something juicily sinful to confess. I certainly felt no remorse, so it seemed futile to ask for forgiveness. But I wanted to challenge the system over something that was considered very sinful by the Church, yet seemed so right to me. I had the sense to realize that this discourse could not happen in or near any of my mother's old confessional haunts. But it was the sixties, and premarital sex was becoming a common urban activity. As I had taken a job in London I made my way to Westminster Cathedral. I might not find a sympathetic clerical ear, but I would at least look for the youngest—and, as it turned out, the handsomest—priest who climbed into the box on a mid-week lunch hour.

"Bless me Father," I said, "but I've got a problem here. Remember the commandment about loving thy neighbour as thyself? Where does the loving begin and where does it stop?" I explained my predicament, namely that I believed in the Catholic way—I was, after all, still learning the organ and singing in the church choir, and organizing numerous fund-raising activities— and that it would be very difficult for me to leave the Church over an act of love. Was that what was expected, I asked, since I didn't want to have to play the hypocrite and crowd his confessional every time I made love with my boyfriend? I was taking a rather defensive tone with him and so his answer came as a surprise. He told me that I had not done anything wrong if I felt right about what I was doing, if I loved this man. If I might one day marry him (I murmured an affirmative), and if I was not harming anyone else by my act, then he couldn't see that I had committed a sin. On my way out I remembered to thank him—in actual fact I think I blessed him, and instead of the prescribed five "Hail Marys" and "Glory Bes" I said the whole rosary in praise and gratitude for him, and then headed, like a storm trooper, through the carved cathedral doors into life.

For the men I interviewed and talked to, rebellion against their religion took the form of political rather than sexual activity. Suddenly the Church was recognized to be a right-wing body with manipulative powers, in material as well as spiritual matters.

Andrew, a young man in his early thirties who is now a priest, remembers when he was fifteen and living in Boston. "Religion became distasteful to me. I came from a traditional Catholic family and the Mass had always been important to me— I felt I gained something from prayer, and my time there. But suddenly I found I was leaving the church angry every time, because we rarely got a Homily or a good sermon, we got a preaching about money. Most people in the neighbourhood put up with it. It was the common joke—you know, how much is Father going to ask for this week? It was needed to keep up the church, the school, but that for me was the single most dissatisfying thing about the Church. My interest was there, but a vocation—no. I stopped going then—from the time I was fifteen—for about a year. I was so pissed off, so tired of the same routine about money, and I knew the neighbourhood was made up of poor, working-class people who were giving what they could give, but it never seemed to be enough. And that was a real insult."

John, from Montreal, remembers, "It was around '58, '59— I can't remember the exact year—when my parents and I were going to church in Quebec. It was a lakeshore community with an old-time French priest, your atypical diocesan priest who is the dispenser of government largesse in the community, the adviser to the local member of parliament. He was the boss, the 'godfather' of the community. I didn't understand French too well so I would daydream during his sermons, but the day came along when he opened up his mouth and said that we would be damned if we didn't vote for the Union Nationale. No separation of Church and State! Well, that was it—my father said to hell with him and refused to go to church again. My mother prevailed for a while, suggesting that maybe we should try another church. We tried a whole lot of other churches until my father said, 'To hell with it for ever,' and he hasn't been back since. As for me, after high school I still went to church for five or six months while I was going to college. Then one day I sat up and said to myself, 'Why the hell am I continuing?' I've left all of that stuff behind me."

Tony, a journalist from Philadelphia, went one step further. He, in his shy manner, told me that instead of dropping his association with Catholicism by walking away from it, he plunged headlong into a substitution. "I stopped going to confession when I went to university even though I went to a Catholic college. I was introduced there to a whole bunch of intellectual views, and the old moralistic Catholicism of my youth fell away very easily. There had never been much intellectual content before—nothing I could sink my teeth into. And it didn't seem like a crisis to me. I was seventeen and it was time for that stuff to go away. I got involved in rival thought at about the time when a large number of priests and nuns from the school of theology decided, almost *en masse*, to explore psychotherapy. One woman at the school was a lay analyst in the Freudian tradition and she began giving a nun friend psychotherapy, and before long many of the nuns and priests were calling for a new community, based on psychotherapeutic Freudian Reichian ideals. The woman who was leading them was a powerful charismatic type, and the others absorbed her thinking seriously. It was like a cult which also provided a substitute for certain aspects of Catholicism—confession, for instance. Group therapy, the idea of vocalizing your troubles, was attractive. You could have retreats too, and what they called marathons, which were like a purging. You felt that you had become a new person, wonderful and cleansed.

"The reason so many nuns and priests became involved in this group was that it gave them the opportunity to come to grips with areas of interest which the Church traditionally opposed, such as occult practices, the theories of Freud with his sexual emphasis, and Wilhelm Reich too, who was also very anti-Church. There were a few who remained practising Catholics, but the majority lapsed."

One man I spoke to in New York mentioned that he abandoned Catholicism in his mid-teens after his papers from high-school graduation took six months to reach the dean of the university of his choice. He had chosen a non-denominational university which was not associated with his Catholic school. "And it suddenly dawned on me that my high school's continual excuses for the papers' delay were nothing but lies—they had never sent them. I was so naive!"

A male Catholic school teacher I met at a party informed me that he felt so sure of his departure from dogma that on his last day of school he threw his cap in the river and put his boots in the holy water font.

These first major rebellions of youth—male and female—are emotionally based. It is interesting to note that the women so often made their rebellion physical and sexual, and the men metaphysical and violent. But there is anger, frustration, and moral confusion on both sides. Nevertheless, the *Rebels*, I discovered, were usually the first to come to terms with Catholicism in adult life. However, there existed a more common group, who were equally confused but in many ways more complacent than the rebellious. These people I refer to as the "drifters".

*The Drifters* were those among us who, at school-leaving age, seemed to drift away from everything. Their experience was not, overtly, as traumatic as that of the rebels. They drifted from home, they "went with the flow" to university or into the job market or marriage, but their religious confusion was to surface later in their lives. The drifters were, and still are, the group who will openly admit to being "lapsed"—an apt description for religious complacency. However, when I dug deep with them, I found that they remembered the "old ways" of their Catholic childhood as something weird yet romantic. Many spoke of their dislike of the new ways—or at least what they'd heard about modern services and broader tolerance of outside religions. They liked the Latin Mass. They believe that the Church had all the answers at one time, and now doesn't have them at all. In some ways, too, they are inclined not to take personal responsibility for their own beliefs as Catholics, since they don't particularly think they should have any, beyond what they were taught. They are perhaps, ironically, the group that the Church would most welcome back.

Paula, now a young mother of three children, was an only child in Chicago, and eighteen years old when she began drifting. "My father was Episcopalian but my mother and I used to go off every Sunday to morning Mass. I went without thinking—automatically—and I only stopped going when I went to college. I suppose I had had enough of it, but it just became easier not to go. I still go when I go home to see my mother—perhaps three or four times a year—and I enjoy it then. It still means something to me, but it wouldn't if I went every Sunday. It's nice to go back—it's familiar—a sort of nostalgia."

Lyn, the novelist and the victim of the radish incident in India as a child, also drifted away, but with a fear of retribution: "I had a visual idea as a child, which I have found is quite common among people who have grown up Catholic, that the soul is like a white lozenge and every time you do something wrong you get a black mark—like when your lungs have become discoloured by tobacco and the doctors hold up the X-ray to try to frighten you into stopping smoking. But I remember the day when I did not go to church and the ground did not open up—and all of a sudden the fear melted away. And then it became my own choice as to whether I should go or not and, well, I'm not going to get up on a Sunday morning when I can stay in bed and have breakfast and read the newspapers."

I was a drifter, but I drifted in instead of out. As soon as I had got the sexual bit squared away with the Church, I didn't at the time have many more complaints. I became more actively involved in running the choir and learning the complexities of that magnificent instrument, the church organ. It distracted me from any theoretical worries I might have had. I was lucky in that our parish priest was intelligent, enquiring, and rather good fun, and gave me responsibilities within the parish. I wonder now if I would have remained in Catholic practice if I hadn't been so lucky in my early association with the clergy—with the priest who first introduced me to the organ and another, a friend of my mother's, who gave me the opportunity to perform at a big wedding in London.

But to most, it seems that the real religious education begins at home. Some Catholics claim that there is a sort of Christian wisdom which they received from their parents. Over and over again, the same message comes through—by setting a good example, parents have a fundamental effect on their teenage offspring.

My mother was the greatest help to me, because she showed, through her own experiences, that the inclusion of the laity in spiritual decision-making was essential. But I seem to be the exception. During my research, I found that men generally claimed to have been religiously influenced more by their mothers, and women by their fathers.

49

Father Andrew from Boston, who stopped attending Mass in anger over the sermons requesting money, was brought back to the Church by his mother.

"My mother was a significant force. She had left the Church years before over my brother. He was an altar server and had done a lot of work for the parish, building a little daily chapel and things like that. He got seriously ill with a kidney disease and was hospitalized for four months, but the parish priest never went to see him. It was a very traumatic time for us—my brother was supposedly dying, although he pulled out of it—and my mother stopped going to church. I would sometimes question her about it and she would tell me that it was her decision and I would have to wait to understand it. She eventually returned, although it was because we had moved to a different parish. It took a while for her to heal, but she returned. So when I was going through my crisis, she didn't lay a heavy trip on me, but then she began to question. We finally talked about it seriously and I said I couldn't understand how she could go to church. 'It is an insult to sit there and listen to that garbage. We don't hear anything about the Gospel—all we hear about is money.' She would let me blow off steam—which was very wise of her—and after a few sessions at which my father said, 'I don't listen to that shit. I just go because I like to go,' my mother said after supper one day, 'You know, one day you are just going to have to grow up.' She said, 'Did you ever hear the expression, you are biting off your nose to spite your face?' 'Yes,' I said, 'but what do you mean?' She said, 'Don't you realize that whoever is in the pulpit, whatever kind of fool he may be, is only human?' Yes, I thought, I can deal with the fact that I have limitations but not that *they* have personal limitations. It was an eye-opener for me because it tempered my idealism, and it helped because after a while I decided that I was being stupid—after all, I was missing not going in some respects, I was missing the prayer, the music—I was being spiteful. So within a month or two I went back."

Tess, from Dublin, spent a few years living and working in North America as a doctor. She intrigued me as she seemed to have come to terms with Catholicism—she'd made her choices and stuck by them. I asked her a bit about her background. What emerged was that her faith had been strengthened by her father, who is now deceased, not by any priest. But if she had taken one experience in her teens too seriously, and not listened to her father, she might have ended up seriously doubting her Catholic affiliation.

"I was in England at the time—I was working there during the holidays—and I went to church now and then. At the end of the holidays I got stuck—I had nowhere to stay for four or five days before I went home to Ireland. So I went round to the local church and asked the priest, did he know somewhere I could stay for four or five days? And he threw me out, he said he didn't want any wanton women around. I couldn't believe it. All through my life I had been led to believe that priests were only kind. Suddenly I met one who was not, and I was very angry. I took out my hatred and fury on the Church. But my father said I was stupid to judge an entire religion by one person. He said, 'You can't find good people everywhere.'

"My parents were both very strict Catholics. They always went to Mass and we always said the rosary in the evenings. My mother was certainly not as strong a Catholic as my father was—he usually went to Mass every day. But he was no hypocrite; he practised his religion and didn't expect you to practise his religion in the same manner. He did get very upset, though, when he found that I was not even going to Mass on Sunday, and used a rather nice ploy, which I fell for in those days—'If you don't go you'll influence your younger brothers and sisters.' So I went!

"I certainly would say that I got most of my religion from my father despite the fact that I got all my Catholic teaching at school. He was my symbolic figure—the man leading a good

Catholic life. And I think he was more Christian than Catholic, which is why I didn't run into problems with him.

"As a result, I related more then, now too I suppose, to the image of my father than to God the Father. My father was the most tolerant person in the world, and I always knew he would forgive me for anything. Through him I gained a strong inner faith in myself that helped me in times of trouble."

Frances is now a Catholic junior-school teacher in Canada, separated from her husband, with two small children at home. We settled into a sofa in her family room to talk as one of her kids plonked away on the piano.

"Both my parents were baptized as Catholics, both born in Italy. But my father's father was staunchly anti-Church—he would have nothing whatsoever to do with the Church. In fact my father had to walk his sisters down the aisle because his father wouldn't go into a church. My father carried the same ideas throughout his life but he wasn't quite so rigid. He maintained that he believed in God, but he just wasn't thrilled about the fact that the Church would come knocking on the door asking him for money when he couldn't even feed his family. He was raised in America during the Depression and times were very difficult. He never went to church and consequently he didn't have my sister or me baptized. He sent us to a non-Catholic school, but always taught us to live by the golden rule, 'Do unto others as you would have them do unto you.' He really was that kind of person who never did anything un-Christian to anyone—he lived according to a Christian code. Now that I have converted, through marrying a Catholic, I find myself teaching the children in my school many of those things my father taught me—a particular attitude to life which is still not emphasized as well as it should be in the religious courses we teach children."

These are all people who had a Christ-like figurehead at home, who were given evidence of that "image and likeness" we were instructed to instil in ourselves but so infrequently witnessed around us. One or other of their parents exemplified a down-to-earth, no-fuss attitude towards their faith. They were healthy, human, and positive, anchoring the spiritual in the everyday.

But there comes a time when parental influence is less prominent in the development of an individual's own attitude. I remember the speed with which the rebels rebelled, while the drifters drifted on. But in the midst of all this spiritual adolescence, a new group emerged—whom I'll call the "pretenders".

*The Pretenders* are those who said they had had it with Catholicism and didn't want to hear about it any more. But unlike the drifters, who just wandered away, the pretenders hurled those many years of indoctrination as far away as they could. They believed they were shaking themselves free, while in fact they were only putting off what would have to be done later in life—coming to terms with their early religion. They may, like the drifters, find their Catholicism rises up to surprise them when they least expect it, when they are totally unprepared and assume—and even hope—it has gone away for ever.

I have known many pretenders, and find that on the whole they call themselves atheists. Some are happy about their decision to shut the door on Catholicism, others are not. This latter group find the process of probing their consciences and talking about it extremely difficult. They hardly know where to begin. I believe that we all—pretenders, drifters, and rebels—need to get onto the road to understanding Catholicism today, in order to come to terms with it at some point in our lives. The longer we postpone the journey, the tougher it will become.

Spiritual maturity can, after all, only be gained through experience, not through innocent supplication or unquestioning obedience. It can be gained by educating the conscience, and to do this we have to go right back to the beginning, to childhood— because it is only when a child's powers of reason appear, when it stops crying when it's hungry, messing when it wants to, sleeping when it needs to, and becomes aware of the power of its own personality and character, that it can take command of its own life—because it is at this critical point, where the ego wakes up and takes over, that we are truly capable of sin.

# 5

# THE DAWNING
# OF CONSCIENCE

"Be babes in evil, but in thinking be mature."

— I CORINTHIANS 14:20

Every Catholic educated in the Catholic system whom I talked to said that there was hardly any discussion of the existence, let alone the power, of personal conscience. It was, and still is, viewed as an adversary of the Church, because it permits individual interpretation of doctrine. Conscience was referred to purely in ecclesiastical terms and suggestions were made to us children regularly that ours was there as an intermediary for the Devil, rather than a more holy messenger.

Conscience came into play when we started to think for ourselves, and to make choices: the choice to go to church or not; the choice to have sex outside marriage; the choice not to confess it or to cease going to confession completely; the choice to use artificial birth control and the choice not to feel guilty about it. Having the ability to choose is the first sign of maturity—and for young Catholics a welcome necessity in the journey to independence and personal redemption, not just the sacred redemption we thought was the only way.

But the sins of our childhood were unfortunately to follow us to adulthood. We had been educated that way. When we were young we knew that "Don't" meant we would be punished if we went against what we had been taught was right, and we weighed our choices based on the severity of the punishment.

Unfortunately, all too often we still do it now. One friend I know has deprived herself of receiving the sacrament of communion for ten years because she lied to her parish priest (she actually told him she lived in another parish so she could be married by the priest of her choice), and she views this as a mortal sin. She has left it so long now, without confessing, that she is prepared to spend the rest of her life doing penance for the lie. Such a situation is the saddest of all cases. There are people who have emotionally tortured themselves for years over imaginary sins, who feel that it would also be a sin to seek absolution or simply advice since they would then be guilty of "using" the Church. They know, too, that hypocrisy is another sin. Many have inherited an inferiority complex and, understandably, a large measure of guilt—guilt which becomes a permanent state instead of a temporary emotion.

I recall what Father Jones, in England, said on the question of sin.

"On the one hand we need to heighten our awareness of its real evil. The ruthless pursuit of self-interest can and does disrupt the lives of others. It is so easy to fool ourselves and say, 'What else could I do? I have my own life to lead. I must put my own happiness and welfare first.' On the other hand, false fear and false guilt can undermine our confidence in God.

"The evil in grave sin is doing or intending to do something which is completely incompatible with the love of God. If one is merely reacting to what the Church says, then one may be rejecting the Church, but it doesn't necessarily follow that one is rejecting God Himself. Such a reaction is similar to the child who disobeys his parents, and is told it is a sin."

Original sin is supposedly behind us, but original sin is the sin we can most readily identify with. It is the sin of being human and questioning—plucking apples from forbidden trees, enjoying the taste, and wanting more of the same. The Church recognizes that our human nature is inclined to evil—there is the "darker side of the personality" which Christian philosopher Carl Jung believed makes us weak-willed. In Roman Catholicism sins are given categories. A venial sin—the most common kind—is defined in the Catechism as a serious offence against God, but is less than a mortal sin, of which every Catholic is acutely aware. In the Catechism both venial and mortal sins are clearly indicated. Under venial are included "impatience, uncharitableness, lies that have no serious results for anyone," and under mortal, "willful murder, adultery, the theft of a considerable amount of money, and lies that do serious injury to others". There is also a chunk of definitions on temptation being the evil voice, warning that when tempted we should pray to God for help to overcome it.

In my own life I have always defined sin as a regular affliction, an everyday temptation which in the short and long run is bad for me. In my case it is usually associated with self-indulgence. I have an excessive nature, so moderation requires some self-sacrifice. I am partial to overwork, but I wouldn't consider that as sinful as a vain, lazy bake in the sun for three hours to darken my skin. I don't like alcohol much so I'm saved from the bottle, but four slices of cake at tea would be a sin of greed. And there is always evidence of my not thinking of others' feelings at some moment in the day.

James Joyce defined sin in his novel *A Portrait of the Artist as a Young Man* as "an instant of folly and weakness", but this type of sin cannot possibly be an act against the love of God. Is a mistake an evil, iniquitous, ungodly wrong? Most Catholics still look to what the Church has defined as God's pleasure or displeasure, rather than thinking it through directly themselves. The Seven Deadlies are worthy of examination:

envy
pride
anger

lust
covetousness
gluttony
sloth.

But how can we be given the choice of behaving in a sinful manner or not, without knowing how to recognize the warning signals? The sins of anger and envy are in themselves destructive, but how can I define *real* anger and *real* envy as they relate to myself without having experienced them? And how do I differentiate between lust and love without practical knowledge? Hans Küng said, "The real deadly sin lies in selfishness, in man's egoism." Yet there is a thin line between *selfishness* and *self-interest*. Looking out for one's own interests is a natural, healthy human instinct, as long as it is balanced with a constant care for others' interests and needs. Without that balance we become selfish, a state of mind that leaves no room for the consideration of others' feelings, and one that obviously excludes God. In such matters, personal conscience must be our spiritual guide.

The following is an account of an Irish friend of mine, Ruth, who learned quickly.

"I decided I wanted to steal, just to see if I could. It began by mistake, really. I was buying odds and ends in a shop, and I put something in my bag and handed the cashier three things, and I didn't realize until later that I had got this thing for free. And suddenly I thought—'Gosh, I could steal!' It never dawned on me before that I could or that I would want to. I remember for about a week or two I then deliberately stole—you know, any old thing—there was no reason for it, it was just to see what happened, to see if I'd get caught, to see if I'd go to hell—to see if I could gamble, I suppose, and I remember towards the end of it thinking, 'Suppose I start stealing from a little shop?'—as I was stealing from big shops, I had argued with myself that they could write it off—'Would that be right?' I felt that was wrong because it might be a family business and I would be ruining a little man as opposed to a company or whatever, but then I thought, 'Supposing I had a very wealthy friend and she had thousands of silver napkin rings and I wanted one—after all, they would never miss just one—but I would be damaging the friend, because if she ever found out she would be upset that I would think so little of her that I would steal from her.' You can easily see something is wrong if it is going to hurt a person because they can't afford it. That's terrible in itself. But then I came to the realization that in fact it doesn't matter who you steal from because you are belittling yourself in the end—you're wearing down your 'right and wrong' because once you start stealing from big places you can soon work your way down to stealing from your own mother."

The formation of a moral self had begun for Ruth. She pushed herself to the edge of the abyss—she stepped out to see if she would fall, and something else happened. She found that in her rebellious act against her Catholic background she was actually hurting herself the most. She experienced a first lesson in morality, and developed her conscience.

Since most Catholics I interviewed seemed to be as much confused about their consciences as anything else, we attempted to define exactly what we think conscience is. However, personal morality is just that—"personal"—and one person cannot interpret another's personality. All the same, it is essential at least to get in touch with your feelings and try to clarify the voice inside you—the conscience—so that moral judgements can be made to your own satisfaction. Thomas Aquinas called the conscience, aptly, "the mind of a man passing moral judgements", but what about the definition of it in terms of Catholicism? I quote the following from *The Catholic Catechism*, by John A. Hardon, SJ:

> Conscience in the strict sense, however, is the action
> of the practical intellect deciding whether a particular,

proposed operation is good or bad, here and now. It is the conclusion at which reason arrives after duly applying the principles of morality to a specific course of action.

But the conscience is also not purely intellectual. It is wound up too with our emotions, causing us, in many cases, to possess a sort of schizophrenic conscience made up of the emotional and the rational side by side. The question is, can one endure without the other? I don't believe so, as there surely must exist the authoritative (and non-authoritative) voice within the conscience, otherwise the conscience would cease to have any effect and would be just a matter of taste, of personal likes and dislikes. Some theological works I have read on the subject state that the conscience should be certain in making a decision. But when we are on the road to adulthood, at a time when it is assumed we are developing mentally as well as physically, it is understandable that we may make mistakes, since the conscience itself may not be fully formed—or, for that matter, informed.

Our consciences need to be educated to serve us adequately. Unless the area of the conscience is worked at it will become dull, with no ability to discern between right and wrong, as when we were children.

The Church has little sympathy today with the idea of personal judgements, or variations or formations of the conscience of any kind. The old wisdom maintained, for example, that through the enforcement of regular Mass attendance and religious rules a light would eventually go on in your conscience—if you hung in there long enough, wandering aimlessly to confession and communion. This may be the case for some Catholics, but any questioning Catholics I have found believe very much that they are responsible for their own destinies—and the knocks along the way.

In coming to terms with Catholicism, the education of the conscience ranks high on the list of "must dos". After all, the Catholic Church is not "the way, the truth and the light"—the inner voice of one's being is, and to any Christian, that is God. And it's a matter of recognizing the twinges, the muddle and the messages, instead of fighting them or ignoring them.

When I was young and impressionable, in London in the late sixties, it was fashionable to attend meditation classes. The whole experience was unsatisfying for me, perhaps because I needed more than just plain sitting and relaxing and getting in touch with my feelings. I felt the similarity between meditation and prayer: both require silence and both offer comfort from repetition. To me, though, praying is not an easy task either, especially when I am reciting other people's words in prayer.

Many I have talked to find that reciting the "Our Father" is more gratifying than anything else—one priest suggests dwelling on the actual words and their meaning. I, like some others, prefer a mental prayer—a sort of conversation with Christ—since I don't find prayer recital a satisfactory formula. A lot of Catholics find it hard to pray, since they find no meaning in the communal prayer at church, and in the past no time was given for the promotion of creative prayer—perhaps because the Church saw this as a formula for developing individuality outside the Church, and also for a life separate from parish community—a life which, to the Church, is not satisfactory and therefore not readily condoned. Yet it seems to me that to develop personal strength and self-discipline it is vital to be able to get into the habit of examining one's conscience at home instead of in a pew, a few minutes before confession, as we did as children.

I read in Gerald Priestland's book *Priestland's Progress* an interesting example of personal prayer, where a woman he knew rose every day and said, "Good morning, God, I'm here," and carried on a chatty conversation with Him throughout the day. She also felt that God's presence is revealed through music. I must say that my moments of reflection—when the subconscious works the chaos into some order—occur when I am gardening: hoeing out the weeds from around the plants, sowing new seeds in the spring, planting bulbs in the autumn. In some ways I get caught up then in the renewal of the seasons, and feel that there is life in what I do. I feel the same when playing the piano and, at times, the church organ—the piano I use to clear my head of the mix and stress of everyday business and personal affairs (Bach is good for that), while the organ is more for glorification, with its great power of sound and its extraordinary sensitivity to temperature and environment. But there are those days when no order emerges even if I would like it to—the fugue seems to be in more of a mess than me, and the trumpet voluntary inappropriately sombre, summing up the state of my conscience at the time. Nothing is plain sailing. Between the clear days roll in the fog and mist, the highs and lows of my moods. At these moments I find my conscience plays tricks on me, and it is then that a mediator can come in handy. By a mediator I mean a chat with a close friend, time with a good book, or just a sit in the park or in a church pew. There is confession too—if you've found a priest you can respect and confide in. One priest I spoke to said, "Because of the changes in the Church, confession has taken on a new dimension—a good dimension—because it is not considered necessary to go regularly, as before. The new penitential rites are useful as they give time for examination of conscience, rather than concentration on the getting in and out of the confessional. There is prayerful time spent, and when people pray, something happens. Through personal prayer people can shed light on a problem, if they are in trouble or in real difficulty. Though sometimes prayer is not the perfect solution."

A talk with a religious can be an effective way of realizing the lost voice of one's conscience, and for a Catholic it is a cheap alternative to the rates of the psychiatrist's couch. And it is no

62

longer necessary to be anonymous, or take the old form of lip against ear, either side of the grille, unless you want to.

Joan, now a very liberal Catholic, who stayed with her faith after rebelling against her father's orthodoxy, remarks, "Sometimes I need some sort of outward reconciliation as opposed to an inward one. The method I use is to see an old friend who is now a priest, and we sit down and have a drink and talk. I tell him where I am and what I've done—where I think I have gone wrong—and maybe at the end of it I will ask him to give me absolution, or not, but I really believe in the personal interchange on a one-to-one basis."

"Whatever you ask in prayer, believe that you have received it, and it will be yours." This is what the Gospel tells us. But prayer can also be a source of guilt, because many pray only when they need something. How many times can you ask for things you desire, for pain to be taken away? Perhaps it would be better to put the desires in order of priority so that you resort to requests only when you get to the end of your tether, like Elizabeth.

"As I'm an actress and in and out of work I am always having to listen to the stories of my more successful acting friends, about parts they got. I heard one day from a friend of mine who lived on the other side of the country, who was predominantly a singer and couldn't act her way out of a paper bag. She sent me a letter when I was feeling down, typing my face off at a rotten, lousy temp job. It was full of the joys of spring, this letter. She had a singing contract, she was working here and there, and the crowning thing was that she had got this role in a dramatic play for three months. I was so mad. I looked up at the ceiling and said, 'God, give me a break!' I shouted it, and two days later I got a part in a play which brought me a lot of recognition."

I rather like this incident as it illustrates what good can come from being angry, not only with one's circumstances but

63

with oneself, and even with God. But when asking for something in prayer, Catholics do have an appealing array of characters other than God to choose from. In *The Catholic Catechism* John Hardon points out:

> The important thing in any form of prayer, however, is an awareness of whom we are talking with and in whose presence we are; it is far less important to be literally conscious of the phrases we pronounce and less still of the meaning of the words we express.

When I questioned Catholics about whom they pray to, a great number paused for a while to think. The two main choices were God the Father and Jesus Christ; very few mentioned the Virgin Mary, although I find old priests rather like to toss the "Hail Mary" into their Masses, which perhaps shows her popularity among men of advanced age. She was of course human, and although she is hard to identify with unless one wants to dig into the symbolism of holy motherhood and the strange notion of the Immaculate Conception, she's likeable, and probably her purity and subservience are misunderstood. And if her image is one that today's Western women find difficult to relate to, perhaps we should be grateful to have any women to pray to at all! The saints—the favourites are Jude and Anthony—sit fairly high up on the Prayer Parade, and then Francis of Assisi, the Apostles, Bernadette. They too were human, and so supposedly possess some hidden secret to redemption, although they are usually called upon to perform acts of magic. I remember two incidents worth recounting. I'm particularly partial to St. Anthony myself, the patron saint of lost causes and things. I rather like the look of him, and the feel of his presence. He is generous too with his talent, since he must be extremely busy finding lost articles for distraught Catholics all over the world. He still manages to work the occasional miracle for me. I lived once with an art dealer (non-Catholic) who, on his return from Paris, found that the airline he was travelling on had misplaced a Renoir painting he was transporting home. He arrived at the door of our apartment, tie askew, eyes like those of a madman. The only consolation I could find in my frantic attempt to calm him was to order him to his knees in earnest prayer to St. Anthony. I assured him that it was futile for him to sweat further, and told him to leave St. Anthony to his own devices. I promised him, confidently, that he would find the painting—all in good time. This calmed him down and we managed to go out to dinner and talk about other things. Six hours later we telephoned the airport to find that the painting had turned up. My friend was running out the front door when I called him back. "There is one thing my grandmother always taught me about St. Anthony," I said, "and that is to remember to thank him"— at which he fell to his knees again, this time in the hall by the open door, with eyes closed tight and hands clasped to his breast, just at the moment our neighbour walked by carrying a bag of groceries. He eyed us suspiciously ever after.

The other time was when a Jewish friend of mine called me on the phone and asked if I would intercede for him in finding his wallet. He'd heard that I had a good success rate with St. Anthony. I told him that he didn't need me since he could pray to him himself, and my friend humbly asked if that was all right— since he was a Jew. I said I couldn't see any problem, as long as he was serious in his request and remembered to thank St. Anthony when the wallet turned up—which it did thirty minutes later, in the restaurant where he had previously searched every nook.

An advertising executive I know in New York found herself at the altar of the statue of St. Theresa—the Little Flower—in a Manhattan church at lunch time. She had always been fond of the Little Flower and she stopped to light a candle. She liked churches, but she'd been a drifter, and had not been to Mass for about twenty years. An old woman came up to her in the church, dressed in rags, and said that if she prayed to St. Theresa for five days running, the saint herself would send her flowers. She decided to do it—she had nothing to lose—and on the sixth day a large bunch of roses arrived at her apartment. The note that came with it was from her mother, who lived abroad and whom she had not heard from for quite a while. The note read, "I saw some beautiful roses today and was reminded of you." She cried, made her confession, and returned to Catholicism wholeheartedly. "It was a little warmth in the centre of the harsh reality of life and I then realized how much I had missed it all."

One American bishop told me that veneration of the saints is perfectly natural. "People sometimes need a human intermediary to help them pray to God." But it helps, I find, to be intimate with one's intermediary—to know that he or she understands. Devotion to saints began soon after the death of Christ, when Christians were killed for their beliefs and religious practice. Some of the early martyrs are well known to us, such as Peter, who was allegedly crucified upside down, and Stephen, who was stoned to death by the Romans. Canonization—the Vatican's stamp of sainthood, usually for performing a miracle or two—is still in existence today. But to me the term "saint" is subjective— the dictionary defines it as "a good sort, good example, idealist, salt of the earth", and I know quite a few of the uncanonized variety. These people have had the confidence, the thoughtfulness, and the intuition to reach an understanding of the human dilemma. They possess the knack of making the complicated simple. They need not be Catholic martyrs, nor deceased miracle workers. But when they do pass away—like Tess's father—one is left in adoration of the memory of their human spirit. I do quite frequently have short conversations with Granny since she died (she was not inclined to long ramblings when she was alive), and I request her opinion on problems which are particularly troubling.

Tess likewise continues her discussions with her father, since his death. "It's not a psychological exercise," she says, "it's merely a case of 'What do you think of this, Daddy?' as though he were still alive. And when I've done something wrong I turn to him for understanding."

We all grapple with our own consciences in our search for the truth within. We search for answers on personal morality, in the hope that we can see clearly the route we should follow. But some people find it hard to take the time to do this—to seek the solitude necessary to think quietly. Or perhaps they are just afraid to face their own consciences straight on. Life can be full of commitments of other kinds, like family and career. Paula from Chicago, who works at home bringing up her three children, said to me when I asked about her conscience, "I wonder if I have a conscience, actually. I suppose I must have one. I really don't know about the spiritual side. I suppose because I look after children all day it sort of gets buried. There just isn't the time for me, being pulled in all directions—even at church on Sunday they are screaming in the aisles. There's never any peace." I realized then that I was in the luxurious position of being able to have some peace in my own life. Being alone for long periods of time, I find the quiet rejuvenating—it is when I feel a spiritual presence in my surroundings.

Human peace must mean contentment, being at rest with oneself—not all the time, but at least some of the time. Moments of peace are essential in our daily lives to restore equilibrium, to help us reevaluate our consciences and our deeds. Such reevaluation is a process we all have to go through continually— the search for our own personal morality, and our attempts to grapple with whatever it is we find. Prayer is a way we can assure ourselves of peaceful moments even in times of trouble.

I remember invaluable advice I once received from an old priest about conscience and prayer. He said that he sits quietly for fifteen minutes a day listening to God, hearing God speak to him. He suggests trying this at home, like daily exercises, first for two or three minutes, then working up to longer periods as one develops the discipline and the skill. And learning to listen *is* a skill, an important part of prayer. A conversation with God can be a valuable two-way activity. I have a particular fondness for the well-known prayer of St. Francis of Assisi—it's a reminder of what I should strive for at times when I run out of topics of conversation with God.

Lord, make me an instrument of thy peace...
Where there is hatred, let me sow love;
Where is injury, pardon;
Where there is doubt, faith;
Where there is despair, hope;
Where there is sadness, joy;
O Divine Master, grant that I may not
so much seek to be consoled as to console;
to be understood as to understand;
to be loved as to love;
for it is in giving that we receive;
it is in pardoning that we are pardoned;
and it is in dying that we are born
to eternal life.

# 6

# LOVE AND SEX

"Let us love one another; for love is of God."

— I JOHN 4:7

Recently, when I visited my parents' home in the Surrey countryside, I accompanied my mother to the local church for Mass,
and picked up the parish bulletin. These bulletins look the same
the world over now. There's a space for the order of the day and
week, the times and dates of the Masses, which poor departed
soul is being prayed for; and then there's the display advertising.
I am always dismayed by this, as I thought Christ lost his temper
at the merchants who hung around the holy place of worship, and
here we are with them advertising their services right in the middle of the religious notes! The advertising is usually followed
by general advice on the day's gospel, or a personal message,
depending on where we are in the ecclesiastical calendar. That
Sunday the message's headline ran: "As a Teenager Should I Follow the Church's Strict Teaching on Sex before Marriage or My
Own Conscience?" It went on:

> On the subject of sex before marriage, the Church, in
> the eyes of many people, is indeed "strict". I'm not sure
> that "strict" is a good word: I think "serious" would
> be a better one. The Church treats sex *seriously*. She
> regards it as a most precious gift from God. And, as
> with all valuable gifts, it's to be used carefully.

The realization that sex is a precious gift—by which we are given the power to create another human being—prevents us, inevitably, from using the gift casually. Christ's teaching reinforces a fact of experience: that "making love" is a sign of our unconditional and total commitment to another. It is not enough to say, "I love you—but only within certain limits." True love is for ever. And that means marriage.

My mother shifted in her pew. I know she believes I am beyond redemption in that department, having never married and having had more than a few healthy relationships since I was in my teens.

I grew up, like a lot of my contemporaries, with The Beatles' hit song "All You Need Is Love" ringing in my pubescent ears—a love, we believed at the time, that could only be found through sexual activity. It was a young love, as naive and simple as the stuff of romantic novels, not the self-sacrificing love that one learns about later in life, that enables you to put yourself in the other's place, and consider the needs of your neighbour over yourself.

If I had, while growing up, taken the Church's message to heart, if I had not decided that it had no part in my lovemaking, I would have been one of those teenage marriage statistics— barefoot and pregnant at the altar. By now I would probably be divorced, playing the annulment game while destroying a few other lives along the way. Without sexual experience how could I have discerned between young infatuation and mature love? But the Church officially forbids sex before marriage, and many were forced to downplay their sexual inclinations—wondering at the same time why they were doing so. Those of us who decided to break that particular rule then discovered that we were faced by another dilemma: whether to risk pregnancy or defy the Church's ban on the use of contraceptives. We found ourselves on a moral merry-go-round.

Only a few days before I read the Sunday message at my mother's church, I had interviewed a priest in London who had said, in reply to my question about adolescent sex, "I neither condemn it nor do I approve it. I stand aside from it.

"I once had a couple who came to me and they clearly intended to marry when they could, but they were both students and they were both on grants. And they said, 'What do we do? We love each other deeply, but if we marry we lose our grants.' I felt that there was something worthwhile going on between these two people, and the only thing that was stopping their marriage wasn't a lack of willingness on their part to marry, but the fact that their finances prevented it. The economic reality, if you like. I also saw that if they continued refraining from intercourse, the strain might prove too much and make one of them turn to someone else because of their settled agreement not to sleep with each other. Someone else might be willing! So I pointed out to them that in the early Church it wasn't necessary for a marriage to be witnessed by the Church; this only came later, and for very good reasons. If a couple, for instance, had a child, it was easy to claim that they had committed themselves totally and they were married, but it was also easy for a man or woman who didn't want the responsibility to deny it. And so the Church then came to the view that the commitment must be witnessed, and that is what a priest is in a marriage—a witness. He doesn't marry people; they marry each other, and they minister the sacrament to each other.

"I think that was a very reasonable position for the Church to have taken. But given the circumstances of this particular couple, and the fact that they were obviously trying to do the right thing in good faith, I advised them that I thought they should sleep together. I happened to see them six months later and I asked them how it was working out and they said 'marvellously'.

I try not to look at this as a black and white thing, but to look at the situation in each individual case."

The teachings of the Church itself on sex before marriage, or sexual expression between consenting partners, are indeed restrictive. The Church does not readily recognize that there can be physical love, and varying kinds of love, outside marriage. Love requires the Church's stamp of approval, and this takes place through the sacrament of matrimony.

## Love and Marriage

Pope Paul VI's Encyclical Letter *Humanae Vitae* was issued in 1968 and is still referred to as the Church's official word on the duties of married people and on the matter of birth control. Its publication caused quite a controversy among Catholics at the time, and a number of lay people and clergy left the Church over the dispute of right of conscience over official teaching. Within it the Pope defined the "characteristic" marks and demands of conjugal love, noting that "it is of supreme importance to have an exact idea of these":

> This love is first of all fully human, that is to say, of the senses and of the spirit at the same time. It is not, then, a simple transport of instinct and sentiment, but also, and principally, an act of the free will, intended to endure and to grow by means of the joys and sorrows of daily life, in such a way that husband and wife become one only heart and one only soul, and together attain their human perfection.
>
> Then, this love is total, that is to say, it is a very special form of personal friendship, in which husband and wife generously share everything without undue reservations or selfish calculations. Whoever truly loves his marriage partner loves not only for what

he receives, but for the partner's self, rejoicing that he can enrich his partner with the gift of himself.

This physical and metaphysical monogamy, conjugal love, is also described in a 1965 document of the Second Vatican Council, *Gaudium et Spes*, "Pastoral Constitution on the Church in the Modern World", as "Authentic married love" which "is caught up into divine love and is governed and enriched by Christ's redeeming power...." It is understood that two people who love each other can be worthy of "special gifts, healing, perfecting and exalting gifts of grace and of charity" from God only if they enter the sacrament of matrimony witnessed by a Catholic priest, in partnership not just with each other but also with God.

The argument given is that "the intimate partnership of married life and love has been established by the Creator and qualified by His laws, and is rooted in the conjugal covenant of irrevocable personal consent." A Catholic married couple "are no longer two but one flesh" (Matthew 19:6), and have an "unbreakable oneness between them", an "undivided affection" and "witness to faithfulness and harmony". There is emphasis on the need for sacrifice to attain this perfect state of heterosexual union, a relationship sealed in the name of God, whose help, we are told, is acknowledged and will be there if and when the stresses of everyday life become too much.

For many Catholics today, the argument that sexual love can only be countenanced within marriage is difficult to accept. The Church, using its power to interpret divine law, through papal documents takes upon itself to set out what love is, with no tolerance for variations of any kind. I, and many of those I have talked with, acknowledge that a serious understanding and respect for marriage are essential. I do not dispute this with the Church. It is because I view marriage seriously that I still remain unmarried. But if the sanctity of marriage is to be preserved, with all society's pressures, premarital relationships should not be frowned on or made sinful.

As I have not met a man I can honestly say I could live with for the rest of my life while remaining sexually and emotionally monogamous—nor found one who has been interested enough to convert me—I prefer, in my conscience, to be true to my feelings. Like most Catholics, I have respect for the Sacraments, including the sacrament of matrimony. It would be an unforgivable lie and an abuse of the seriousness of a religious commitment for me to enter lightly into an arrangement which demands so much not only of oneself, but of another. To me it is not a sin to love freely, if one has matured enough to understand what love is, but love and a vow of marriage do not necessarily go hand in hand. In marriage, there are a number of areas beside that of love which have to be considered—the needs and motives of the other, the reasons for marriage, the desire for a family, immigration, legal requirements. But Catholicism is a traditional, disciplinary religion which promotes the fulfilment of family life as the primary motive. A number of Catholics I know who have married happily are that way, they claim, because they did not feel guilty about indulging in sexual intercourse before marriage. And a number claim that since marrying they have felt an enormous weight of personal responsibility lifted from their shoulders—that weight being the sexual and emotional experiences they had to undergo before they met the "right person".

A commitment to another outside the sacrament of marriage can also spare partners the distress of refuting vows made before God—for a far more serious dilemma arises when married people turn elsewhere for their sexual and emotional gratification, because the maturity needed for the commitment of marriage was not there to start with. It would be preferable to live with someone, even to have a family, without marriage, than to marry, have children, and then decide that you cannot live up to what you vowed before God as witness.

But if any love is to last, there can be no doubt that it will need help—not so much from the Catholic Church, but from the God within us, from the personal strength required to endure the bumps and scrapes and misunderstandings and breakdowns of communication along the way.

It was Paul who said:

> Love is patient and kind; love is not jealous or boastful; it is not arrogant or rude. Love does not insist on its own way; it is not irritable or resentful; it does not rejoice at wrong, but rejoices in the right. Love bears all things, believes all things, hopes all things, endures all things.
>
> I Corinthians 13:4–7

It is not up to Rome to tell us whom we should love, how we should love, and what we should do to express it.

## Variations on a Theme

How can we categorize our feelings of love—a word that is itself so open to abuse?

Love is an entanglement. An entanglement of two people— or more; an entanglement of mind and body, and an entanglement of emotions, which cannot and should not be assigned areas of acceptability or non-acceptability. The Church defines conjugal love as "authentic", but what happens to the alternative forms of loving? What happens when two people of the same sex fall in love? How can restrictions and rules be the basis for feelings?

If turning against the love of God is a sin, as we recognize it to be, then it is foolish to believe that loving another, partly or completely, is going against His will.

And what of the lives of members of the clergy, who have to remain celibate? With rare exceptions—such as the married Anglican minister who converted to Catholicism, and was ordained as a married Catholic priest in 1987—the Church still denies its clergy the solace of sexual love. But today, more than ever before, priests and nuns are questioning the rule of celibacy, the old order that marriage to another person will conflict with one's ability to love all people, will conflict with one's vows to God. A nun, after all, becomes a bride of Christ when she makes her vows. And Christ Himself, who was not only God but also man whom God made sexual, exemplified ideal, celibate love. Unmarried, He did not restrict His emotions to one person to the exclusion of everyone else; from what we know of Him, He seems to have been less interested in sexuality than in spiritual love for others. Two nuns I spoke with in Pennsylvania told me of the enormous aptitude their celibacy gives them for loving. Free of the limitations of sexual and emotional monogamy, they are able to be more generous to others.

But a growing number of men and women are giving up their clerical posts to pursue other ways of loving. And many celibates I interviewed told me that their fantasy was to get married and have a family—as Anglican clergy are able to do. The state of celibacy can be frustrating and restricting. What happens when the love of God gets chosen over the love of another human being? What if human love is ignored or unrequited?

There are numerous stories in literature of one person's pursuit for perfection, in giving his or her "all" to God at the sacrifice of human love. One of my favourites is the history of Abelard and Heloise—two intellectuals of the twelfth century, and as famous a pair of lovers as Romeo and Juliet. As a young girl, Heloise fell passionately in love with her private tutor, Abelard, renowned throughout France as a brilliant philosopher. She became pregnant, and gave birth in hiding to a son. They married in secret. There were several reasons for this secrecy— marriage was not only contrary to their philosophy, but it was also not in Abelard's interests. As a married man he would never be able to obtain high office in the Church—and the Church was in those days the only career open to an intellectual. But despite the secrecy (or perhaps because of it) Heloise's uncle, in fury, sent a band of his servants to break into Abelard's quarters in Paris, where they attacked and castrated him. Carrying the stigma of his injury, he became a monk, while Heloise entered a convent, against her wishes but at Abelard's request. The letters between them are famous, hers for her eloquence, passion, and wisdom, in her deep and mature love for him, his for his pontificating on the Gospels, which was his way of providing comfort, he thought, for their loss of physical love. He rejected Heloise as a woman, discarding human love in favour of the love of God.

Great loves and great lovers have been a source of passion throughout the ages and have given us many examples of humility, selfishness, daring, and surrender. One of the most moving novels of the twentieth century, Graham Greene's *The End of the Affair*, is the story of a man who loses the love of his married mistress when she slowly withdraws from him for God. The variations on this human theme seem inexhaustible. Some of these loves, however, are more famous for their involvement with one of the Seven Deadlies (such as greed, lust, jealousy, and revenge), since love and sin are often found closely entwined.

As Catholics, we are constantly plagued with guilt over the sexual act—perhaps because it is so pleasurable, and we were too often taught as children that sacrifice and suffering and abstinence are the true way to redemption. The clergy and the Church were always there, reminding us of our sinfulness, of our abuse of our bodies, of our disobedience, of our humanity.

It is, I suppose, obvious where this distaste for free sexual expression is rooted. The fact that the Catholic clergy take a vow of celibacy (established by the Church as far back as 305 AD) gives the sexual act itself a particular prominence, making it appear unnatural and sinful. Through time there have been reports of incidents where clerics mutilated their own genitals in an effort to avoid temptation. In *Sex and the Penitentials*, Pierre J. Payer concentrates on the foundation of sexual ethics in the early Christian Church. I found the following canon amusing, yet disturbing:

> If a bishop commits adultery with another's wife [he shall do penance] for twelve years, three of these years on bread and water, and is to be deposed; a priest for ten years, three of these years on bread and water, and is to be deposed; a deacon and a monk, for seven years, three of these years on bread and water, and is to be deposed; a cleric and a layman, for five years, two of these on bread and water. The aforementioned are to be deprived of communion. After the penance has been completed, they are to be reconciled to communion, for they shall never approach the priesthood.

Masturbation has always been a safer alternative, but since the act does not promote procreation, merely sexual gratification, it too is viewed by the Church as sinful and falls into the category of the deadly sin of lust. Finding a theological basis for this decree is difficult, however. There is no biblical reference to masturbation itself except for Onan, made famous for spilling his seed on the ground in Genesis 38:8–10:

> Then Judah said to Onan, "Go in to your brother's wife, and perform the duty of a brother-in-law to her, and raise up offspring for your brother." But Onan knew that the offspring would not be his; so when he went in to his brother's wife he spilled the semen on the ground, lest he should give offspring to his brother. And what he did was displeasing in the sight of the Lord, and he slew him also.

78

One wonders if this small incident was solely responsible for the Catholic Church's condemnation of the act of masturbation. For it is difficult indeed to translate masturbation itself into an act against the love of God. And one cannot argue that the act harms anyone.

One middle-aged American priest told me, when I asked how he survived the lack of sexual activity, "When the feelings are too strong, I masturbate—that's the bottom line. I try to be honest about it, and I don't see it as sinful. There has to be a release sometimes—that is essential. If I am not getting creative support from work or in my relationships with others, then I feel dissatisfied, and I find relief in masturbation. But it isn't human contact, I know, and that is frustrating."

I found that almost none of the Catholics I talked to were concerned about whether masturbation is sinful or not; for them the questions revolved around the consequences of sexual intercourse and free love on the one hand, and the struggles of emotional commitment and sexual monogamy on the other. Catholic dogma proclaims in no uncertain terms that the mind should control the needs and functions of the body and keep it from temptation. I liken this to a car without gasoline or petrol, or machinery without power. A balance must be present to fulfil the needs of the adult body, and sexual activity is very much a part of that balance.

The mind and the body are one, and sexual intercourse provides a vital means of unspoken communion between two people.

I also see the sexual experience as one of the ways in which God speaks to us, in a physical way, not only through the conscience.

A male or female orgasm is biological energy released and revealed and as such it has its own spiritual dimension. It gives us mortals a glimpse of the subconscious "completeness" of mind and body, and allows us to possess a beautiful sense of well-being and love.

Sexual intercourse is the one expression of human love without limitation, and no one can fully understand how God speaks to us without knowing this association with others. A flirtatious brush of hand or lip, a brief glance, a warm smile, a long kiss, the lead-up to the act of sex itself, is up to the individual to interpret. We are given free will so we can choose our means of communication.

And we take the chances of the personal consequences.

One woman I know said she felt that she had damaged herself spiritually when she "used" a man to satisfy herself when she had the sexual urge. She believed that she had sinned against herself, but it was a private matter and not something she felt she wanted to talk about or disclose to a male cleric through confession. She had now learned by experience about the weakness of her own flesh, and she could not see why any church should get involved, or "stick their collective nose into my private parts", as she put it.

Sex itself, I believe, is not sinful unless it damages yourself or someone else. But to damage another or yourself deliberately is to act against all the laws of God. A clear example would be if a carrier of a sexually transmitted disease, who was aware of the possibility of passing it to others, did not refrain from sexual activity, or provide, where feasible, the necessary precautions, or even refer to the risk.

The advent of the terminal disease AIDS (Acquired Immune Deficiency Syndrome) has made us all more conscious than ever of the need for responsibility in sexual matters. The persecution of those afflicted, including recent reports of priests with AIDS being treated like lepers by their orders and left to die alone in unfamiliar communities, has been appalling, and the condition itself has been foolishly and unrealistically described in self-righteous, apocalyptic terms as a scourge of God.

Catholic homosexuals have already borne a number of "scourges". They have been struggling with rejection from the Mass and Eucharist for years, but in October 1986 they were officially outcast by the Vatican through Cardinal Ratzinger's letter to the bishops of the Church, where he cited homosexual inclinations as a "strong tendency toward an intrinsic moral evil".

A Catholic acquaintance, who is very traditional in his thinking and believes that the only place for sexual intercourse is within marriage, noted politely to me in a recent conversation that "the Church, you see, has been right all along. If we'd followed their advice we'd not be in such a mess now."

I strongly disagreed with him. In condemning and pointing fingers at our neighbours' sexual preferences, we can hardly be exalted as Christians, who respect, understand, and have compassion for the different needs of others. Laying down laws and circumstances in which human beings can express their love will not lead to a world of purity without pain, suffering, sickness, and disease. Choosing celibacy out of fear of the physical and emotional consequences is surely not the answer. Sexual feelings cannot be swept under the carpet. Instead, the beauty of physical expression between two people, heterosexual or homosexual, married or single, Catholic or Protestant, should be acknowledged and upheld. It is the means we all have to contribute to our love of another, and to enhance our own strengths and spirituality.

As Edwin Clark Johnson says in his book *In Search of God in the Sexual Underworld*:

> ...if our sexual activity is going to lead us beyond ego into participation with the divine creative activity, if it is going to enhance our lives and keep us young and vital as we grow mature and wise, we must feel glad that it remains ever present in our consciousness.

# 7

# THE BODY AS TEMPLE

"Earth and the heavens are before our eyes. The very fact that they
are there proclaims that they were created, for they are subject to
change and variation.... 'We exist,' they tell us, 'because we were
made.' And this is proof that we did not make ourselves. For to make
ourselves, we should have had to exist before our existence began.'"

— ST. AUGUSTINE

We, as Catholics, learned at school that our bodies are given
to us by God, and that their preservation is our responsibility.
When I was a child, I imagined my inside was like a big red
vessel which held my soul and, occasionally, God's heavenly
host. This vessel frequently gathered grime and black muck but
it was easy to clear—it got sucked out by some spiritual vacuum
after a visit to the confessional. Later, throughout my teens and
early twenties, my body was simply something to fill up with
plenty of food, drink, and then the birth control pill. Taking the
pill was so easy: just pop it in your mouth and your worries
would go away. Somewhere in the back of my mind I knew,
like many of my Catholic contemporaries, that what we were
doing—taking the pill and having regular sexual intercourse with
a variety of partners—was definitely not acceptable in the eyes
of the Church. But that didn't stop us. Most of us stopped going
to Church instead. I still went to Mass but I refrained from
communion. Offering the Body of Christ the company of the Pill
seemed insulting.

## Contraception

It is ironic that a Roman Catholic invented the birth control pill.
John Rock was working on a chemical solution for infertility

when he came up with the most popular drug of the sixties—causing quite a stir in Rome. David Yallop's bestseller *In God's Name* gives an interesting account of the papal politics at the time. Yallop describes the dilemma the Vatican faced in preparing an official Church statement barring artificial contraception, searching through the Old and New Testaments to find some theological evidence to support their position. The problem was, there wasn't any. And at that point the Church should have left the matter alone. But public pressure was building, and the media wanted word. So, like Paul centuries before, pressured by the Corinthians and the Romans to come up with statements on issues that concerned them, the Vatican published *Humanae Vitae*, and gave its reasons for doing so:

> No believer will wish to deny that the teaching authority of the Church is competent to interpret even the natural moral law. It is, in fact, indisputable, as our predecessors have many times declared, that Jesus Christ, when communicating to Peter and to the apostles His divine authority and sending them to teach all nations His commandments, constituted them as guardians and authentic interpreters of all the moral law, not only, that is, of the law of the Gospel, which is also of the natural law, which is also an expression of the will of God, the faithful fulfillment of which is equally necessary for salvation.

With the publication of *Humanae Vitae*, the Vatican took an official stand against all forms of birth control except abstinence and "rhythm". But the statement came too late; there was already more political haggling to be heard among priests and bishops than divine wisdom. Many Catholics had already made up their minds about preferred methods of birth control, having listened to their consciences. So why did they take *Humanae Vitae* so seriously at the time? Why did clergy leave their orders over it, and why did Catholics around the world throw up their hands in despair?

From the perspective of the eighties, it seems like a translation of an ancient text from around 400 AD, not a clarification of life in 1968, when man was preparing to walk on the moon, and space exploration and genetic engineering were advancing rapidly. As a guide, *Humanae Vitae* would have been helpful to those who felt that uninterrupted childbearing was necessary for their economic well-being, as in the past when children provided labour on the farms; or in the less developed countries of the Third World, where many births are still necessary to ensure a family, because the child mortality rate is so high.

*Humanae Vitae* upholds the complete union of two in marriage, and preaches the perfection of natural—that is, unimpeded—intercourse with procreation as the intention. A sexual act "which jeopardizes the responsibility to transmit life" contradicts not only the purpose of marriage but the will of God, the Encyclical states. God's grace is bestowed on a Catholic married couple to help their love endure for each other, and to interfere with its purpose "is to contradict the nature both of man and of woman and of their most intimate relationship". This husband and wife never fight, squabble, or try to juggle a suitable time for sexual intercourse, let alone understand that they might find beauty in abstaining on certain days (the rhythm method). Their children do not hamper their unity or transcend it; their affection is never selfish, the needs of each are purely for the other, and they possess, as they have been instructed, "solid convictions concerning the true values of life and of the family, and...they tend towards securing perfect self-mastery." Of course, it is assumed that they are both Catholics—tried and true—who find regular Mass attendance no problem with children at their feet. And should one partner not interpret their commitment the same

84

way as the other, or be lazier in the effort to comply—making the road a bumpy one—they are advised:

> Let them implore divine assistance by persevering prayer; above all, let them draw from the source of grace and charity in the Eucharist. And if sin should still keep its hold over them, let them not be discouraged, but rather have recourse with humble perseverance to the mercy of God, which is poured forth in the sacrament of Penance.

I am reminded of what Joan told me when we talked about her background. She said, "A lot of the problems I had in my marriage, especially concerning sexuality, came from my parents. My mother was very cold. She had child after child after child, and I remember her saying how hard it was not to be able to kiss her husband good night in bed because she was afraid of the consequences. Her attitude was always very negative towards sexuality and there was very little physical warmth at home. She never hugged us or even touched us as children."

Today, *Humanae Vitae* is not considered an infallible document by a number of clergy I know. Father Jones from England said to me, "As far as contraception is concerned, we have a state of armed truce in which it's fully acknowledged that there are two points of view, and neither side is giving way. So, to me, there exists no teaching within the Church on contraception. There can be no teaching if the Church itself is so deeply divided." Another priest said, "I regard the issue as neutral in the sense that a carving knife is neutral. You can use it for good and you can use it for evil."

But we must not adopt birth control blindly. We must give thought to the physical damage, if any, that we may be doing to our bodies, our temples. It is difficult to know what long-term effects certain "wonder drugs" and chemicals may have on our health. Thalidomide is a good example, in which combatting the nausea of the early stages of pregnancy led to a large number of children being born with severe physical handicaps. Now, more than thirty years after the invention of the Pill, medical reports suggest there is evidence that it is damaging to the body in more ways than we ever perceived possible. A chemical contraceptive such as the Pill abuses the natural laws of our bodies—by releasing estrogen into the bloodstream, it simulates pregnancy and therefore prevents the monthly release of the egg. Among the reported side effects are inflammation of the vein walls, thrombophlebitis, acute myocardial infarction, and thrombotive and haemorrhagic stroke. Some doctors have warned that we have not yet seen the real side effects of the Pill, nor what serious conditions it may cause in the future.

No one would refute that we have a responsibility to protect ourselves and our bodies, but despite this, casual experimentation with drugs to improve the body's functions and heal its disorders has become a common practice in our times. The introduction of drugs to the human body could, in the long term, impair its natural functions. So could the insertion of foreign objects such as the IUD (Intra-uterine Device). For myself, I have never been happy with the idea of cluttering up my insides with foreign objects—they get in the way of the natural cycles. Nor have I liked the concept of sterilization; I would find it very hard to make the irreversible decision to become barren. But I've known many men and women whose consciences have told them that this process would be right for them. And in some instances—where the woman's health was likely to be endangered by pregnancy—the Church itself has granted a special exemption for sterilization or other forms of birth control.

The rhythm method—abstaining from intercourse on days when conception is most likely—is in keeping with the body's natural functions and is the only birth control condoned by the Church. However, it is an unreliable and risky alternative—the failure rate is reported as over 20 per cent per year. And how natural is it anyway to be poking around in your vagina with a thermometer every day, and feeling the lining of your underwear crotch to determine whether one day's discharge is thicker and more elastic than another day's?

Although coitus interruptus has been practised by Catholics for centuries, it too is perceived by the Church as an unacceptable intervention in natural destiny, as are natural blockage methods like the condom and the diaphragm. Coitus interruptus has practical weaknesses as well—most people agree that it is not only risky but a frustrating form of birth control. But these days the condom in particular seems heaven-sent. What a simple, safe invention it is; it can help prevent not only pregnancy but the spread of many sexually transmitted diseases.

But I have read in recent reports that in some North American Catholic schools teachers and clergy, while trying to illustrate the use of the condom as a safeguard against the spread of AIDS, have to do so without actually condoning its use as a method of birth control. A hard lesson to give! So many teachers go ahead on the assumption that young people need to practise birth control even if it (let alone sex before marriage) is forbidden by Rome. Most feel that withholding health-care information from young people for the sake of a doubtful morality would be the graver sin.

The publication of *Humanae Vitae* caused distress and confusion to Catholics struggling to come to terms with the pressures and freedoms of modern-day life. Many wish that, instead of banning birth control completely and citing it as interfering with God's natural laws, the Vatican had had the wisdom to take a more reasonable stance. It could have issued warnings about certain methods of artificial birth control, those which may contribute to malfunctions of the body, instead of passing judgement on individuals by insisting that they were participating in evil and therefore turning against the love of God. By condemning outright the use of artificial contraceptives, the Church showed no compassion and no understanding of the need for family planning. By rejecting even the blockage methods which cannot hurt the body, like the condom, diaphragm, or cervical cap, it can only have contributed to the rise in the much more serious alternative—abortion.

But there is now a bigger issue that we all have to face, one that the Church should be far more occupied with than warnings to Catholics about the evils of masturbation, the use of the condom, the taking of the Pill, or the insertion of the diaphragm or the IUD. In its self-assigned wisdom to interpret natural law, it has had to take a stand against advancing scientific experiments and medical breakthroughs such as the fusing of ovum and sperm in a laboratory dish. The future now holds the very real possibility that human beings will be able to determine biological destiny. Can the Church force a halt to such medical progress?

Rome might answer,

> The law of the Lord is perfect,
> reviving the soul;
> the testimony of the Lord is sure,
> making wise the simple.
>
> Psalms 19:7

But the precepts of the Bible on such new moral issues are, not surprisingly, lacking relevance in the modern world. There is certainly some wisdom in reminding and guiding us to progress in union with our biology, and to conceive in a natural way. But not everyone who can conceive wants to and not everyone who wants to can.

*In Vitro Fertilization*

The Church feels, and with some good reason, that we, as human beings, should concern ourselves with the preservation of human life, in all its guises; and that we should not flout God's will by interrupting the natural course of destiny. A document published in 1987 by the Vatican, "Instruction on Respect for Human Life in Its Origin and on the Dignity of Procreation", states that:

> The natural moral law expresses and lays down the purposes, rights and duties which are based upon the bodily and spiritual nature of the human person. Therefore this law cannot be thought of as simply a set of norms on the biological level; rather it must be defined as the rational order whereby man is called by the Creator to direct and regulate his life and actions and in particular to make use of his own body.

It was not that long ago that test-tube babies were science fiction, but now they are reality—and institutions around the world are experimenting in the direction of cloning and genetic manipulation. Medical expertise is developing and becoming more sophisticated in an astonishingly short period of time.

But Rome also observes that "what is technically possible is not for that very reason morally admissible", and cites, as an example, the transmission of human life itself:

> The transmission of human life is entrusted by nature to a personal and conscious act and as such is subject to the all-holy laws of God: immutable and inviolable laws which must be recognized and observed. For this reason one cannot use means and follow methods which could be licit in the transmission of the life of plants and animals.

In other words, the natural way is the only way. According to the Church, there is no alternative way. The body is our temple: it is the place where the woman's eggs develop; the place where sperm, in the man, and ova, in the woman, have life and together, in sexual intercourse, may fuse to create an embryo; the safe haven where the foetus grows and develops until, approximately nine months later, a human being is born.

The Church views this process of creation as a gift from God. God is the third party in the "specific and exclusive acts of husband and wife". From God comes the gift of love and from that the gift of life. And while I disagree with the Church's refusal to condone intercourse except between married people, I do agree that God must have something to do with procreation. We do not have the power alone to conceive; we have the choice to prevent it happening but when we want it to happen we cannot always control the timing. That is the mystery of life—God's will.

Now it seems that this mystery and this authority have been denied to some extent by none other than man himself, caught up in the excitement of creating a Garden of Eden in the laboratory. The Church argues vehemently against scientific experimentation when it comes to *in vitro* ("in glass") fertilization because "various procedures now make it possible to intervene not only in order to assist but also to dominate the processes of procreation." If there are natural blockages in the body which prevent pregnancy occurring, for example, surgery to correct the situation is permissible. But when a couple opt for insemination they throw natural destiny to the wind, just as they do if they choose to use methods of preventing pregnancy.

The whole process has opened a Pandora's box for the Vatican. For one thing, acquiring sperm for *in vitro* fertilization requires an act or two of masturbation, which the Church does not condone. Also, not one but a number of ova have to be removed from the woman over the course of a few months, in case one experiment doesn't "take". Then if a zygote (a cell produced from the sperm and ova) is formed, "the biological identity of a new human individual is already constituted", states "Respect for Human Life", and

> Thus the fruit of human generation, from the first moment of its existence, that is to say from the moment the zygote has formed, demands the unconditional respect that is morally due to the human being in his bodily and spiritual totality. The human being is to be respected and treated as a person from the moment of conception; and therefore from that same moment his rights as a person must be recognized, among which in the first place is the inviolable right of every innocent human being to life.

Grave concern exists for the destiny of zygotes that are discarded, or frozen, traded, or experimented on. Above all, the third party contributor is not God but the lab technician, doctor, or surgeon who arbitrarily decides which zygote will be implanted: "He sets himself up as the master of the destiny of others inasmuch as he arbitrarily chooses whom he will allow to live and whom he will send to death and kills defenceless human beings."

The whole scenario introduces a powerful human dilemma: how can we advance scientifically and medically, yet marry this growth with spiritual maturity and awareness?

The Vatican states that "Science without conscience can only lead to man's ruin."

But again the necessary question is, whose conscience? Rome's conscience? A collective conscience based on Christian values? Or the individual conscience?

Should we not be exploring how we may best safeguard the dignity and spirit of human beings, their physical and mental health? Many concerned doctors involved with infertile or sterile couples believe that they are helping them in their need, making their wishes come true, healing their pain. And indeed they often are. But we have barely begun to understand the physical and spiritual toll such medical advances may take on those who participate, and to know what sort of permanent psychological damage may come about in a future of human beings conceived under the bright lights of a laboratory. Maybe none at all—but as most of us were conceived naturally, it's difficult for us to put ourselves in a test-tube baby's shoes. Had we been conceived in a dish, would our attitude towards our family be different? Would the bonding to one or both of our parents be the same? Would knowing that you were wanted so much that you were conceived through scientific means bring on a fear that you might never be able to live up to your parents' expectations? And what then would be your understanding of God's will, of natural destiny?

In the future, the population of our world could well be made up of people conceived in test tubes (whether the offspring of one or both of their parents or from donors other than their adoptive parents), and surgically implanted in the wombs of surrogate mothers. It will certainly be a different place from the one we know and belong to now. And so in the new world of scientific developments it is imperative that we examine our consciences to decide if unnatural conception is acceptable to us, and to determine if the disregard for the sacredness and privacy of our bodies is not a violation of our temples.

And medical advances will not cease as time progresses. In the not-too-distant future it will probably be possible, not only to choose which zygote is to develop, but also to tinker with the genetic makeup of the child to come—to change or eliminate characteristics deemed "undesireable". I do believe it is essential, however, that we observe the laws of nature, that we not become so caught up in the pursuit of scientific perfection that we lose touch with reality, with disease and retardation, with the imperfections of the world in which we test our Christian will, our capacity for love and sharing. If we are not careful, there will be no joy at all—only a search for self-satisfaction, a grabbing, materialistic society, people who pay any cost to have the child they feel they are entitled to. If conception cannot take place inside the body, then that fate should be accepted. The mystery of life, I believe, is sacred and should be observed. It is not just a human being's existence and its rights that we tamper with, but the innermost mystery of all, its spirituality, its soul.

> We are all biological creatures, and the greatest of us
> know that and work with biology, not against it.
> *The Madness of a Seduced Woman*,
> Susan Fromberg Schaeffer

*Soul Searching*

I feel it would be beneficial at this point to contemplate the soul. The soul has always been a mystery—its existence hardly acknowledged (as it cannot be pinpointed under a microscope, or anywhere else). Yet the soul, and the question of when it actually comes into being, is at the heart of the difficult discussion surrounding the creation and preservation of human life.

We live in an age when biological mystery is not fashionable. Professor F.D. Maurice, a theologian from King's College, London, suggests in an interesting article I came across in *The Times* of London that there is a movement towards a new contemporary thinking about the makeup of human beings as mere "structures of matter", much as we once viewed organisms in the lab at school. He mentions that we are now "proclaimed to be complete bundles of macro-molecules". This view is shared by the scientist Lewis Thomas in his book *The Lives of a Cell*:

93

A good case can be made for our nonexistence as entities. We are not made up, as we had always supposed, of successively enriched packets of our own parts. We are shared, rented, and occupied. At the interior of our cells, driving them, providing the oxidative energy that sends us out for the improvement of each shining day, are the mitochondria, and in a strict sense they are not ours.

Whose are they, then? Professor Maurice points out that "popularizing biologists" are now concentrating on efforts to dethrone humanity from its old place of spiritual dignity. He feels that the soul is under attack and that the "attackers" see the soul as a sort of "ghost in the machine", "a disembodied entity which is mysteriously connected with the body".

I believe that the soul is the core of the human being. And if we recognize only biological matter, then surely it becomes the most intriguing and valuable property of that matter. Carl Jung believed that God guided us from the centre of our beings and that spiritual truth was a thing "living in the human soul" and not an "unreasonable relic of the past". The answers, as always, lie within ourselves; as a race we can either abuse our spirituality or battle for its preservation.

I found some enlightening sections on the soul in an extraordinary document written by a monk in fourteenth-century England, called *The Cloud of Unknowing* and described as a book of contemplation "in which a soul is united with God". (It is now available in an accessible paperback edition and is a treasure house for any questions on spirituality.)

> ...man, who is the best-looking creature that God ever made, is not made bending toward the earth as all other animals are, but is made upright in the direction of heaven. And why is this so? In order to represent in

physical form the spiritual work of the soul, a work that is possible only for those who are upright spiritually and are not spiritually bent toward the ground. Take note that I say upright spiritually and not physically, for how can a soul whose nature has nothing physical in it be drawn upright in a physical way? No, that never can be so.

Be very careful, therefore, not to understand in a physical way what is meant spiritually, even though it is spoken in physical words such as up or down, in or out, behind or before, on one side or the other. No matter how spiritual a thing may be itself, it is unavoidable that if it is to be spoken of at all it must necessarily be spoken of with physical words, since speech is a work of the body performed by the tongue, which is an instrument of the body. But what of that? Does that mean that it should, therefore, be interpreted in a physical way? Not at all; it should be interpreted spiritually, as it was intended to be.

As Catholics, we are taught that the soul is the recipient of sanctifying grace; it survives us, transcends us, and assumes perpetual responsibility for our human activities. It is the God within us. In 1518 the Fifth Lateran Council proclaimed the soul as "not only truly, of its own nature and essentially, the form of the human body...but also it is immortal" and therefore there is no mortal language to define its path.

Over the years, religious philosophers and theorists have tried to determine exactly where the soul is and when the body is infused with it. It was not until 1869 that the Church referred to it as "created" by God at the moment of conception, and now, much later, Catholics have stuck to this theory when taking a moral stand on the right to life of a foetus. In the mediaeval period, the Church accepted another theory—that the soul entered the foetus at different stages, depending on its sex: forty days after conception for a male, and eighty days for a female. At other times it was believed that the soul was first present when the mother experienced the "quickening" movement of the foetus in its fourth or fifth month. But as there are myriad such assumptions, we must obviously all come to our own conclusions.

I believe it happens right at the beginning—at the moment of conception.

One evening a while ago, I caught, purely by accident, a television program called *The Miracle of Life*. This is a documentary produced by Swedish television and is a spectacle of micro-photography magnified half a million times.

Through extraordinary techniques, the viewer becomes a voyeur as we witness conception itself. We are first given sneak previews of what is going on in the scrotum: things are noisy in there as the sperm become active, busily preparing for their journey. The sound they make is like that of a large jet in the sky. (I had little doubt that what I was witnessing was a very masculine activity. I remember once having a conversation with a woman doctor about the battle of the sexes, and she came up with what must surely be the final statement on the subject. "The difference between men and women," she said, "is purely and utterly biological. The men give out, the women take in." Is that why women take so much responsibility for sexual consequences?)

Meanwhile, back on television, we've slid into the penis. We are now floating around among the red and yellow folds of the inner flesh. I remember that I was thinking how it all reminded me of sunset skies in paintings by the Old Masters— the religious scenes—when, to my astonishment, I noticed some sins in there—little black specks. But the narrator reassures us that they are calcium deposits. In the distance is a mysterious black hole, and suddenly white fluid, like rushing water crashing over rocks, or a bird in flight, surges by us and is gone.

Cut to the vagina.

The same interesting fleshy folds as in the penis, but these serve as little ledges for the sperm to rest on. We learn too that the vagina produces a nasty fluid which kills a lot of the sperm on entry; evidently the sperm are viewed by the female body as the enemy. But this is apparently nature's way of making sure the strongest and mightiest of sperm win through in the race for reproduction.

Some of the sperm cannot manage to get going again after their rest, while others motor on past. Some are stupid enough to fertilize a normal body cell by mistake. It's amazing that any make it at all! But they travel in numbers and the outer sperm protect the inner ones. Then we're given a picture of the female ova, and it too is enlightening; it is beautiful and dignified. I can see the connection between it and everything else—the planets and the moon, the tides, energy and matter. Here is a greenish-blue snowflake, "the genetic treasure", as Germaine Greer so aptly described it, independent, strong and alone—purely female. Meanwhile, at the other end of the Fallopian tubes, the group of feisty sperm races on. Along the way they have survived a grab bag of biological hurdles, and the survivors—like courageous knights breaching the last defence—manage to break the final barrier and fuss about the rotating snowflake. It slowly moves around while sperm penetrate the outer layers of the egg itself.

There is no time for rejoicing and sitting back now, only for getting on with the act of creation—the marrying of cells, of those two strange elements which have finally come together. The head of the sperm erupts with explosive force and pours the genes from the man into the egg. When this happens, the two cells from the man and the woman become one cell—one flesh—and then, within twenty-four hours, that cell begins to subdivide.

While this is going on, the zygote, as it is now called, rolls around in the blue sea of the tube, accelerating with the activity of the new cells which grow and divide, grow and divide within it. As it travels towards the uterus it reminds me not so much of a snowflake but more of a gleaming gold jewel haloed by feathery light—a form within a form, magic itself.

At the end of the program, as we saw the foetus grow, I found myself lost in the wonder of conception. (How the Marys, Magdalens, and Elizabeths of Friday afternoon red-box question time back at school could have benefited from a viewing!) But I realized too that it was only through advanced modern technology that I had been privileged to witness what it is usually impossible to see: the beginning of human life, and how in many ways it was divine, how God had taken part.

That jewel-like embryo was so like the vision I had of my own soul that I could not possibly believe, after that, that the soul of a person could appear at a later point of development. It was all there at the beginning, for me, as it is the centre of our being now.

Before I formed you in the womb I knew you,
and before you were born I consecrated you....
Jeremiah 1:5

## Abortion

The moral dilemmas surrounding *in vitro* fertilization and surrogate mothering are relatively new compared with the years of struggle over the subject of abortion.

The numerous concerns—of a woman's right to choose what is to become of her own body, of a man's right to his unborn offspring, of a foetus's right to life—and the political battles that have been fought and are still being fought over this moral issue, have been written about and talked about at great length.

Catholic men and women I spoke to shared these concerns, yet I was particularly interested in exploring them further with Catholic women who had had an abortion. I have read of many examples of non-Catholic women who felt that their decision to abort was the right one at the time, but who did not expect the loss of the foetus to haunt them as it did for years afterward. Evidently the emotional, biological, and psychological trauma was severe in a number of cases.

Catholics have to contend, moreover, with the fact that they have committed a mortal sin as well. They have not only done what the Church has told them is wrong, they have also broken one of the Ten Commandments: "Thou shalt not kill." The women I eventually found and interviewed were confused about their status as Catholics. They would not confess their abortion, and seek absolution for it, as they believed that their decision to have an abortion was made in full conscience, and that they were therefore, in the eyes of the Church, fully responsible. They had no doubt, given their personal situations, that the abortion was their only solution. Yet at the same time, the gravity of the act itself still hung over them and hampered their religious practice.

Sally, now a mother of two, is in her late thirties and sells property in London. She was twenty-one when she first found herself pregnant. "I was just out of college, and was saving up to go to Italy, and I thought, I didn't want to lose my virginity to a Latin—mind you, in hindsight it would probably have been a better idea! I was living at home since I was working to save money for the trip, and I started dating someone who worked in the same factory. He was short and only came up to my navel, and I managed to get pregnant by him."

I asked her if she had been using contraceptives. "Oh yes, on and off came the condoms, and one got a hole in it. It was one of those things, you know, a quick ejaculation—and oh God, what do we do now? And God in his infinite wisdom answered.

"There was a route. Everyone I knew had, was having, or was going to have an abortion, especially those nice girls at Catholic college. Some were up to the fourth one by my age. And so it was very easy. The only problem was that I lived at home, so my friend Caroline dreamed up the idea of a weekend party—it was just before Christmas and just before I was due to leave for Italy. (It all came at once, so to speak.) So I went up to London on a Friday night—I was living in the country—I had no qualms whatsoever about it. Saturday morning I reported at the clinic. I stayed Saturday night and woke up on Sunday morning, when Caroline came to pick me up. I was two and a half months gone, and it cost £80 out of the Italian savings."

"Was it love?" I asked.

"No, it was lust," she said. "But even if I had loved him, I would have done it. I just didn't want a baby then. I was going to Italy. Of course, once bitten twice shy, so I took the Pill from then on. Looking back on it, I have no regrets, I had no other choice. I couldn't have a child I couldn't love, which would ruin all our lives."

But even though Sally feels no doubt that she was right about having an abortion at the time, she now feels that she is beyond redemption. She was later married in the Catholic Church, during a Nuptial Mass, and in preparation she attended confession but did not confess the abortion. She now says she has feelings of remorse that she cannot practise Catholicism with the freedom she would like, because she has not only—in her own words—"committed a big sin", but she has failed to confess it since, and so considers she has lied to God.

"I wonder why I didn't mention it then, when I had the opportunity? Maybe I wasn't contrite because it was the only thing I could do at the time. It was the only thing to do." She turned to look out of the window, and bit her lip.

We talked together about her spiritual future. She was educated in a Catholic convent and religious practice was important to her. Her husband is now lapsed from Catholic practice, but she still goes to Mass every Sunday and her children attend a Catholic school.

"So do you take communion at Mass?" I asked her.

"I can't, can I?" she replied. "I haven't confessed."

"But surely," I went on, prodding her, "you must deal with this problem sooner or later. If you felt at the time that you had no alternative than to abort, and you still do, and feel no remorse for that, the much bigger problem for you is the loss of communion with God."

"I know," she said, "but what can I do? It's stated quite clearly by the Church that anyone who has an abortion is excommunicated—automatically."

I left my meeting with Sally, feeling sad. It was winter and I trudged along in the cold and dark, finding little sense in the situation. I know of so many Catholics like Sally, who respect the validity of the Sacraments enough not to abuse them, yet live as Catholic outcasts, and could do so for the rest of their lives.

However, were we not taught that the Lord is all-forgiving? American scholar David Mall, author of *In Good Conscience: Abortion and Moral Necessity*, claims that:

> What is right and wrong, including abortion, is not dependent on God's will; however, because of God's inherent nature, He always does right and could never approve of wrong including abortion.... God wants us to be autonomous moral agents because that is our true nature.

If this is the case, then how can Catholic women who have gladly aborted make peace with God and, just as important, with their religion?

I put this question to Father Jones as we talked and had tea together. I asked him if automatic excommunication from the Sacraments meant that one becomes less of a Catholic, or not a Catholic at all.

"It's not a matter of being a Catholic or not being a Catholic," he said. "If you totally cut yourself off from the way of the love of God, you are not a Christian, are you? If one is knowingly and deliberately taking a path that one feels is so contrary to the way Christ pointed out to us—and therefore the way of the love of God—one is effectively cutting the love of God out of one's life. Now, very, very few people ever take a decision on any issue which is seen to be contrary to the love of God and then go on to pursue it deliberately. Only then, when the decision is totally deliberate, when it is an issue which is in your bones, your inner feelings, when you feel your decision is totally separate from the love of God, would it be a grave sin. And no personal excommunication from the Church holds water unless it is as a result of a grave sin. So it wouldn't just have to be abortion. It would have to be a deliberate decision that one is going to take one's own way, and if that excludes one from the love of God...so be it."

But this would be a difficult decision. If one felt right about the decision to abort at the time, with no remorse for the act afterward, would that be in direct defiance of God? I hardly think so.

It is a cruel irony that someone like Sally turned the tables and denies herself communication with God now, because she interprets her relationship with Him solely according to the rules of Rome.

Lorna is a single woman of forty-five who works for a government agency in Washington. She found herself pregnant in her late twenties by a married man with whom she had been having an affair.

"I didn't think twice about having an abortion. Getting pregnant was an accident—I hadn't even contemplated having a child—and I just had to get rid of it as quickly as possible, and besides the situation I was in with this man was hopeless. However, now that I live alone and have no one really special in my life, I sometimes regret this decision a lot. I wonder, for instance, what my now teenage child would have been like, how my life would have been different, fuller perhaps.

"I was a lapsed Catholic—meaning I ignored Catholicism for most of my adult life—but now I find I need it again and I'm trying to deal with my emotions on that, which includes the abortion as well."

I asked Lorna how she was doing this. Does she feel now, fifteen or so years after the fact, that she committed a sin by having the abortion?

"It's not just a question of sinning," she answered. "It's something that goes much deeper than that. I know that I was immature and unprepared mentally and morally at the time to deal with the consequences of either the abortion or the raising of a child. So I didn't make a responsible decision then, but only now, in retrospect, can I see this to be the case."

I was reminded of what Father Jones had said in one of his fireside chats with me on the interpretation of sin: "If an action is followed by regret or remorse, consent could not have been in full. That would be a clear indication that one was acting with a divided mind." And he went on to explain that a woman who has to decide in haste to terminate the life of her unborn child (which it is usually necessary to do, to avoid the medical dangers beyond the first trimester of pregnancy) has little time to weigh the consequences and listen to her conscience. David Mall believes that the rational and irrational are together at play in any decision-making process, and that irrationality in the moral world is much more serious than in the physical world. Viewing the earth as flat and the centre of the universe, for example, is not as tragic a misconception as support for slavery or abortion represents. Moral reasoning is a matter of deep human importance.

Could it be considered, then, that in both Sally's and Lorna's cases the abortions were not sinful? They were not acts done against the love of God, because neither woman was mature enough to make a clear judgement of conscience. Yet if the clocks could be turned back for either of them, with the knowledge they have today, how much easier would it be to decide to terminate or not terminate the foetus's life?

If a child is not wanted, conceived without love by rape or by accident, the possible choices are pretty dismal: either abort that life and put an end to it, or give it up for adoption and never know what has become of it. Both choices go against our natural instincts. But if a choice has to be made, any woman is forced to ask the question: is aborting an easier affliction to live with than giving a baby away?

It has been proved that as soon as most women are aware of being pregnant a strong bond with the baby begins to develop, and many women have stated that after an abortion they mourn greatly, not so much for the foetus itself but for the lost relationship between mother and child. But the decision to abort often arises from a woman's need to steer the course of her own life. Nowadays, it is unfeminist to say, like Mary, "Thy will be done," or to carry the physical and emotional load alone, readily accepting the idea of "selfless love". The feminist message has always emphasized self-development over self-sacrifice. Women have made a vital effort to protect themselves, and not to be servile or helpless; in effect, this has meant being self-sufficient. But there exists only a fine line between self-sufficiency and selfishness.

According to American psychologist Carol Gilligan, women and men differ enormously in the area of moral choice. In her book *In a Different Voice: Psychological Theory and Women's Development*, Gilligan argues that women are inclined to be more subjective and more influenced by their sense of moral responsibility. Their morality is rooted mostly in relationships between people and in the corners of daily life, rather than in abstract moral principles.

It is only recently that men have been invited to attend at births and go to prenatal classes with women. Their role in the process of procreation has begun to be recognized. But because the female has traditionally borne the main responsibility for the child, and because in the past many men preferred it that way, it is understandable if they are not always brought into the decision-making process in the matter of abortion. The few men I have spoken to are upset and feel let down because a woman they slept with decided on an abortion without their having a say. But if the pregnancy was the consequence of a casual sexual encounter, most women would not want to give the man a chance to object.

The difficult, often painful decisions that accompany an abortion have brought with them one important realization: the need for discernment in sexual activity. The question perhaps to ask oneself before entering into sexual intercourse is "Am I prepared to accept the consequences of pregnancy with this person?" Although, unfortunately, this question is, for the time being, more likely to be asked by the woman than the man, it can be more easily answered than "Should I consider abortion, giving up for adoption, or bringing up the child myself?"

These questions can apply to married people as well as singles. Frances, the Catholic convent-school teacher who is now separated from her husband, provides a good case for accepting the consequences of one's actions. "Because I had recently been accepted into the Church, and had been baptized and had made my first confession and communion, I had had no advice on birth control when I married my Catholic husband. He was irresponsible and he really did not want to face the possibility of children. He was very young—we were both twenty-two then—but I was a little more realistic so I practised a pseudo form of rhythm. I got foam and tried to use it only according to my menstrual cycle, and I tried to use it minimally so that my husband wouldn't be perturbed—this settled well with his conscience. But obviously I slipped up on the way. I was really distraught when I became pregnant and was ready to go to the nearest abortion clinic. We had been married only eighteen months and my husband was still a student, in his second year towards his masters degree. I was the breadwinner of the family and had only been working for three months, and you had to work two years to get a permanent teaching certificate—if you didn't you had to go back and retrain. The job situation in teaching was really bad and I was lucky to have been one of fifteen people to get a position on the local board, so I thought the world was going to end. I was making only $7,000 a year—we just didn't have two cents to rub together. We hadn't done anything at all with our lives. We literally had nothing. We hadn't been anywhere, hadn't done anything, and for the whole time we had been married it had been study, study, study, and scrounge, scrounge, scrounge. I know, looking back now, that I did have a nervous breakdown—a walking nervous breakdown, that is. I went to my doctor. He was a Catholic and his wife had five babies running around in diapers. She didn't work and they were obviously not suffering any financial hardship, so I suppose I should have known better than to go to him. But I did, and he said, 'Well, there is nothing you can do about it now and you should have thought about all that before this.' There was no question of an abortion as far as he was concerned, and I didn't know who else to go to.

"I mentioned abortion to my husband and he was obviously upset at the very word, but he didn't offer any alternative either, even 'Don't worry, we're in this together—everything will work out fine.' I got no support from him or the doctor. I didn't feel I got any from my parents or from his either—nobody jumped for joy at the news. I really felt alone. In my mind I was a Catholic on one side but on the other side I was in a situation I felt was hopeless, which is why abortion didn't seem wrong to me at the time. I was pregnant with a child I didn't want, I hadn't planned for, I didn't feel I could take care of, and I couldn't accept the financial burden or the emotional burden. I would be bringing a child into my own narrow world, which he didn't deserve. I really felt that my child deserved better than to be the child of parents who couldn't give him half of what he should have."

Frances, mainly by force of circumstance, had her son. She didn't know where to go for counselling, nor did she know where to go for abortion services. But looking back, she says, "I loved that baby more than anything in the world. I used to cry at how much I loved him and I thought, how could I ever have considered an abortion when he, my son, had turned out to be the only joy in my life?"

But as a result of the problems she had experienced, her marriage suffered and, in the end, her husband left her to cope alone.

## Moral Choices

There is now however a further question which our generation has to deal with. Thanks to technology, we now have the means to determine the cell makeup of the foetus through amniocentesis. What does one do when faced with the knowledge that an unborn child is—or may be—abnormal? How does one decide whether to abort or not?

Elizabeth, now forty-two, is doubtful whether she would get pregnant. "But if I did," she said, "I would have a higher risk of carrying a deformed child. If I found that I was, through an amniocentesis test, I would have to ask myself what effect such a child might have on my marriage. I've had some contact with mentally handicapped children, when I worked temporarily at an institution, but I know that my husband couldn't handle a severely handicapped child. It's easy for pro-lifers to throw stones. I think abortion is murder, but I know that my marriage comes first—it's a sacrament given to me by God, and that would have to take priority."

A newspaper reporter from London who moved to the country to be near her only daughter, who is in her early twenties and institutionalized there, said in a wistful way, "I wouldn't wish it on anyone. My whole life revolves around her, because she will never grow up, will never leave home. I don't think she is happy. Most of the time I ask myself, 'What is the point of her life?' "

The eternal human question. It is not one we can easily answer about ourselves, let alone others. And in many ways it is not a question we are entitled to ask. A close friend of mine told me once that the answer to the question "What is the reason for living?" is "Life", and I believe the quality of that life and the way of that life are not open to human judgement and interpretation.

The pro-life groups promote protection of life from the moment of conception, through birth to death. The Catholic Church's position is uncompromisingly pro-life, and one of its main messages is in defence of the unborn, the right to life of the foetus. It has taken a strong moral stand on the issue and condemned abortion.

But abortion has also become an issue on the political platform. And society is divided not only on the ethical questions; while there is a demand that safe abortion services should be available to women, there is also concern about the long-term effect that the casual destruction of life may have on society generally.

A newspaper editor I know in Chicago, who is Catholic, finds he faces a moral dilemma quite frequently over the abortion issue, as his paper supports a woman's right to choose and to have services available to serve this need. He believes that abortion is morally wrong, but does not allow his opinion to affect his work. His solution is to pass the assignments on this topic to colleagues. I have been put in a similar situation once or twice. Prominent women lobbying actively against government for the availability of good, safe medical facilities for abortions have called me to join them in rallies, conventions, and fund-raising events. I decline because while I know abortion would be wrong for me, I respect the right of the individual to make his or her own choices. For myself, "collective pro-abortion" versus "pro-life" stands diminish beside the dictates of the individual conscience. "The right to choose" confirms that human beings have been created with consciences for the purpose of making use of them. To put the rights of an unborn child before the rights of the mother may not be the only path. Rather we should be asking: how can we be of help to both?

The Catholic Church is in a position to go one step further in its attempt to protect life. Instead of promoting the line that "abortion and infanticide are abominable crimes" (*Gaudium et Spes*), leaving many Catholics to carry the guilt of murder, they might provide an intelligent and understanding service for those in doubt, before or after an abortion. Let them recognize the need for Catholic women to talk to Catholic women about these problems, and find, through the help of nuns and parish counsellors, a way to offer assistance and reconciliation.

One very tired nun, Sister Helen from San Francisco, told me that she and a number of her contemporaries are now the ones who are approached for counselling by Catholics, who usually prefer to talk to women because they believe they can empathize.

"It is amazing how many require moral reconciliation with abortion. We provide as much help as we can, but I feel hampered by not being able to give the formal forgiveness of the

Church, not being a priest. In most cases I would, if I could, because I know how some women have suffered." Instead Sister Helen suggests they go to confession—where they can obtain absolution, from a man—but she adds, "I know that most wouldn't bother. And I don't blame them. Why go through it all again? I know some have privately come to terms with God, though, and go to Mass, but they don't partake of holy communion. You know, we have got to understand that abortion is not a black and white issue. If we are Christians, we, like Christ, must show compassion and provide hope, and a way of absolution."

She rummaged in the drawer of her desk and pulled out a copy of St. Augustine's *Confessions*. "I've been meaning to frame this, but I never have the time." She read it to me instead:

When we love our neighbour by giving him help for his bodily needs, our souls bear fruit in works of mercy proper to their kind, for they have seed in them according to their species. We are weak, and therefore pity leads us to give help to the needy, aiding them as we should wish to be aided ourselves if we were in like distress. This we do, not only when it can be done with the ease with which grass runs to seed, but also by giving help and protection with all our strength. Then we are like a great tree bearing fruit, for we do good to a neighbour, if he is the victim of wrong, by rescuing him from the clutches of his assailant and providing him with the firm support of true justice, just as a tree affords the protection of its shade.

# 8

# THE PRODIGALS

"When you're young, you discover sex. When you're older, you discover religion."

— IRVING LAYTON

While it is often easy for us to pinpoint when our adolescence began, it is harder to define when it ended. Adulthood is a state that does not commence at a particular age, although I remember thinking that when I reached the lawful age of consent I would have arrived. Of course I hadn't. Becoming an adult in all things, including religion, is a long, arduous process, though some manage to make the journey shorter than others. Adulthood, too, is a state linked closely with maturity, and to me in my youth maturity was something you received when your hair turned white. But what is it exactly in spiritual terms?

I believe it is a feeling of inner peace which settles over the rebellious needs of adolescence; when some answers emerge from the turmoil that went before. We need to prove while growing up that we are unique, and different, and independent; we fight against tradition and despise conformity; we prefer chaos over harmony. But after any rebellion comes a need for renewed order, for discipline, for daily ritual and, above all, company. The whole cycle begins again, as we link up with a mate, have a family, and watch our children go through adolescence themselves. We can nod and say "I told you so," or perhaps not comment, understanding that the trials of adolescence are both natural and necessary to each individual in the search for identity. We realize,

111

as well, that our own lives have a history—we have lived long enough to have a past of some significance. For most Catholics, a large part of that past has been drenched in dogma.

It isn't hard to realize, too, that Catholicism is not just a religion but more a way of life. In our rebellion, many of us try to run away from that way of life, as we did before from childhood things, only to find as we look back that what we rebelled against is still very much with us and we are nowhere near spiritual maturity. Just as we are preparing to pass on to our next of kin some codes for survival, we realize that we have not yet come to terms with the frustration and anger we felt against the religion of our adolescence. And what use are we to others, let alone ourselves, when we haven't sorted out our own feelings towards Catholicism? We finally have to be or not be Catholic, and it's not an easy decision to make. Most of us are ill-prepared, with misinformed consciences, to make the decision at all.

Earlier, I raised the idea of the Catholic club. Clubs have always been popular in our society—people need company, they generally like to belong to a home away from home. When we were children at school we were herded into assembly every morning, where we chanted hymns of praise; we joined sports teams and discovered what loyalty was all about. When we were in our teens we joined fan clubs and youth clubs. The individualistic rebellion of adolescence caused a break in the pattern before we were drawn back to the idea of community, of the importance of finding a place among similar-minded people sharing similar goals. Christianity is about the same thing—a group of peoples, which Father Jones earlier described as being the makeup of the "Church". In the Catholic sense the Church is its people, who meet to praise a common God; it isn't a clutch of cardinals who interpret the message and lay down the laws.

Human beings do not generally function well in isolation for any great period of time. If I lived in a remote area of the world, I would belong to a tribe or village; in the city, I belong to the bustle. Teilhard de Chardin remarked in his book *On Happiness* that:

> ...however individualized by nature thinking beings may be, each man still represents no more than an atom, or (if you prefer the phrase) a very large molecule; in common with all the other similar molecules, he forms a definite corpuscular system from which he cannot escape. Physically and biologically man, like everything else that exists in nature, is essentially plural. He is correctly described as a "mass-phenomenon". This means that, broadly speaking, we cannot reach our own ultimate without emerging from ourselves by uniting ourselves with others....

For de Chardin love is the centre of the individual, and itself drives us forward.

This is the Christian interpretation. But the reference to nature introduces a more scientific interpretation of this need to belong. The scientist Lewis Thomas, in his book *The Lives of a Cell*, again sheds light on the balance necessary for human survival in his explanation of human beings' need for company as well as privacy. He begins by comparing ants and termites to human beings. He notes that the individual bee, termite, or social wasp lives two kinds of lives:

> ...they are individuals, going about the day's business without much evidence of thought for tomorrow, and they are at the same time component parts, cellular elements, in the huge, writhing, ruminating organism of the Hill, the nest, the hive.

He goes on to observe that when hundreds of thousands of ants get together and blacken the ground,

> you begin to see the whole beast, and now you observe
> it thinking, planning, calculating. It is an intelligence,
> a kind of live computer, with crawling bits for its wits.

The Church clearly understands the power in numbers. Christ, laying the foundations of the early Christian Church, also knew that his message would spread more quickly if he preached to the masses. The Vatican favours a clamouring crowd to greet the Pope or to attend outdoor Masses—reinforcing each time its powerful religious and political base. We are drawn to a crowd because we either know we belong within it, or are inquisitive enough to see if we'd be interested in belonging to it. There is an excitement when huge numbers congregate to celebrate with one mind in one place. So the individual ant doesn't stay away from his fellow ants for long. Ants and bees are conditioned to live in societies made up of their common species because without them they would die. They need to feed off each other to survive. People are not so very different. We tend to herd together, to find comfort and support in society at all levels, whether it be a club, a crowd, our country. And just as Catholicism bears the traits of a club, so too does it take on the force of a nationality.

Since Catholicism has its roots in Judaism, it is not, I feel, out of place to draw a similarity here between Judaism and Catholicism. The Jew, however, is one step ahead of the Catholic in reaching maturity, in that a Jew knows if he or she is Jewish, and never doubts it. There are of course Jews who are not religious, who choose not to attend synagogue services regularly, but it would be surprising to hear a Jewish person deny his or her heritage. Judaism is, of course, a racial heritage as well as a religion—but Jews also bear the stamp of being the Chosen People. They are brought up to believe that they are in an important sense special. Poet-songwriter Leonard Cohen remarked in a magazine interview:

> I don't think the Jews are the only people who are chosen. The thing chosen for them, though, is a high thing: it is to be a vessel for a certain kind of truth, the vessel of revelation.

The Jew *belongs*—has a place in a delineated community. And in fact so do Catholics, although we hardly admit it. We may not believe we are actually chosen people, but we *are* brought up to believe that the Roman Catholic Church has imbued in us something special which we cannot lose, even if we want to. We're held by an invisible umbilical cord to the body of the Roman Catholic religion.

Lyn, the Canadian novelist, rebelled against the Church but found her Catholic roots again in France, where she spent a couple of years in her early twenties.

"You know, I missed a lot of the ritual. Of course, everywhere you go in France there is some incredible cathedral, and every museum you go into is filled with religious art, and it was very hard to separate what I missed from the Church in terms of the beauty and the ritual and incense. I took great satisfaction in walking into a church in the evening and sitting there quietly. There was also a greater sense of history. Catholicism in Europe makes so much more sense than it does in North America because it is so much a part of the fabric of social and cultural life there. France has an interesting version of Catholicism. The French have adapted it, in their own weird and wonderful way, to suit their attitudes towards life. I like the way they have made peace with all the elements of Catholicism."

Catholicism, as a nationalistic culture in the "Catholic" countries of Europe and in areas of the Third World, is integrated into everyday life. It is less so in the United States and parts

115

of Canada; for example, Lent and Advent are not honoured as periods of preparation and penance in general society, and Holy Week—the highest point on the ecclesiastical calendar, and the Catholic "New Year", if you like—is not even highlighted by social or family events outside Church ceremonies, unlike the Jewish tradition, which gives attention to the solemn as well as the celebratory holidays. In North America, the melting pot for all nationalities, there is a reverence for the Jewish holy days. It is fully accepted that it is not proper for Jews to do business on Jewish holidays, just as it is not proper for Christians on their feasts of Christmas and Easter. For myself, I find I need to feel the solemnity of the Passion of Christ and recognize the symbolism in the Lenten and Advent periods to be able to find reason for celebrating Easter and Christmas at all. In Catholic countries such as France, Spain, and Italy, holy days and feast days are officially recognized. Perhaps that is why Catholics feel more at home in that environment than in England or North America.

"I get a sense that in North America your religion is a separate private issue and has no bearing on the way you live your life," Lyn said, "whereas in France, whether you go to church or not, it is assumed that you are Catholic by birth and have gone through all the Sacraments etc., so there is an ardent 'Church' there. There will be priests in the cafés, nuns on the street—it's all natural and normal—the fabric of society. It's even there in terms of food! I mean, the cuisine in France is much more immediately tied into the religious aspects of the whole thing. There are all sorts of holy days that are cultural and social holidays—they are all tied to the religious calendar and have evolved over a long period of time without interruptions and reformations.

"I felt that I belonged more to the Church there, even though I didn't attend Mass regularly. Catholicism made sense to me at that time in my life. The cultural activity suited me."

Lyn's strong sense of belonging reminded me of the difficulty that some rebels, drifters, and pretenders describe in coming to terms with the culture of Catholicism in their lives, when they live outside a Catholic country. For those of us who attended Catholic school, school was a country. The nuns and priests and Mass were as much a part of our day as schoolwork. But in early adulthood, there was nothing that evident. We had to go and find what was familiar—seek it out. It wasn't visible and there was no focus or central meeting spot for people like ourselves. Mostly we believed that any Catholic church was packed full of the converted—those of the old ways who didn't mind the oppression of the Vatican. We felt they were in there toeing the line, kneeling, standing, and sitting as ordered. We didn't, then, notice the others—those who were starting to look in again from the outside, wondering if they should enter. The Church wasn't offering any room for them. But what it was offering, at least, was the Sacraments—the gifts—and at some point in their lives many Catholics find they miss the Sacraments most of all. The Sacraments, of course, are very much a part of a Catholic's past, and drifters who begin to yearn for the old country, who decide to find their way back, feel entitled to easy access—just by flashing the old membership card. They forget that it is necessary to renew.

For instance, after many years of living together, Lyn and John decided to get married, and they wanted all the trappings of traditionalism for their ceremony. They did not stop to consider the possibility of a need for reconciliation with whoever they believed God to be—Christ or Father. Instead they "returned to Catholicism"—having no idea what they would step into. And they were turned away; they were not theologically or spiritually equipped to break through the red tape of the Catholic order to find a place for themselves within the Church. Their story—the story of two Catholics who attempted to return to their native religion—is long, but worth telling in its entirety, I feel, so I leave it to them to tell on their own.

*John:* We decided that it wasn't worth receiving the sacrament of matrimony unless we knew what we were doing and meant what we were going to say to each other. However, we had got away sufficiently from the Church to forget that this sacrament was wrapped up in dogma. Neither of us was a virgin, of course—we had had our flings in the past—but at least we both regarded matrimony seriously.

*Lyn:* When John and I started living together, we had a good relationship. We were older than average—in our mid-thirties. We were not virgins fresh from holy communion leaping into marriage. For us matrimony was the end of the process, not the beginning. We had a major commitment to each other. I believed in the basic principles: that one enters into marriage seriously; that one makes a commitment, and does not go out of one's way to hurt someone else; that one grows, and cares about one's fellow man. And when it came to getting married, for me the Catholic Church meant tradition. We wanted a ceremony—a public one—to say to our family and friends, "In your eyes we are making a commitment." And the only way to make sense of this was to do it in a Catholic environment, because that was, for both of us, what tradition was—the music, the altar, the ceremony, that it be done in the eyes of God.

*John:* My job is intellectual in nature. And my interest in the intellectual is largely a result of the Jesuit training I received in high school. I had always had tremendous respect for the Jesuits—and I found I somehow wanted to go back and discuss all our concerns with them. I realize now that I still had, subconsciously, an image of a Church run by socratically oriented priests one could talk to, and what we ran into was, of course, quite the opposite.

*Lyn:* I hadn't been to Mass for about fifteen years so the first thing I did was to start researching how to go about getting married. A Dominican priest friend informed me that the first thing is to go and see the priest from your local parish. So we both ambled along to St Boniface's, not having stepped into a church for a while and, in my case, still viewing the priest as a person of great intelligence and authority. We met the priest, Father Jacques, and were taken into his study. He lit up a cigarette, which immediately made us feel good as John and I had often talked about how wonderful Catholicism was in tolerating physical everyday things such as drinking and smoking, compared to the more severe ethics of Protestantism. However, it became quickly apparent that this priest was just plain stupid. We were honest with him, and we told him we were lapsed Catholics—fallen away from the Church for a variety of reasons—and we were now coming up to this milestone in our lives. We realized the importance of our backgrounds and traditions etc. At which point he pulled out literature on the Encounter Weekends for the Engaged. He didn't want to hear from us. He said, "All right, you go and you take these pre-marital classes." And then he added, not with any vehemence, that we would have to start coming to church again. And the first thing he gave us were collection envelopes. I came out thinking this was amusing, but John had a migraine headache.

*John:* It hit us too, in that initial meeting, how totally out of touch we were with what was going on in the Church today. But we were curious. He said that he was not going to be checking on attendance with us, but with the collection envelope, of course, we knew that he was going to be able to. This was the test to prove our sincerity!

*Lyn:* We were getting a bit worried now so we found out through our friends about another priest, Father Lowry, who is a Dominican and interested in alternative Masses. He had done a great deal of social work and was extraordinarily intelligent and hardworking. Now, Father Lowry was the opposite of Father Jacques. He was a Zen priest. He was more interested in theory than in the nuts and bolts. His house was decorated in Danish pine and he had classical music on the stereo.

*John:* I liked him, because he was more like a Jesuit. You felt he was slicing the baloney a little thinner than most people would. His critical question was "Do you consider yourselves members of the Christian community?"—a very different approach from Father Jacques's "Are you active within the local church's

120

organization?" He defined it as, "Are you Christians in practice?" and I found it easy to say yes to the latter question, that yes, I believe I try to run my life as a Christian. I believe in all the fundamental precepts that Jesus Christ Himself laid down, and that Moses brought down from the mountain years before.

*Lyn:* Father Lowry tentatively agreed to marry us after the first or second meeting. The problem was that the parish he was attached to was out in the west part of the city, but he suggested that if we preferred we could get married in a chapel in the university to which he was affiliated. We went to see it and it was beautiful. It had all the elements—everything I expected for my church wedding. We went back and said yes, we would very much like to get married in that chapel. So then we had to go see Father Robinson, who runs the Catholic centre at the university to which the chapel belonged. We felt much cheered by Father Lowry—at least there was one person in the Church who was on our wavelength—and we went feeling less despondent about whether the wedding would ever come off as planned. We went to meet Father Robinson—a large, thick man with white hair who wore an orange jumpsuit with green socks and had a yappy little dog named Basil (he was Basilian, you see) that tried to take your ankle off every time you moved. We expected, after our meeting with Father Lowry, that we would have a similar dialogue with Father Robinson—a baring of the souls. He was at least a priest at the university—and we had expected, to a certain degree, a fairly liberal man. Instead, we had two hours of fire and brimstone: about belonging to a Christian community, about going to church on Sundays, about going through the parish priest for our wedding, and about the chapel. He harangued us, and said he would not have us prostituting the Church just because we wanted a pretty venue for our ceremony— at which point I felt enormously guilty because I had fallen in love with the chapel and he hit a nerve right there. He went on to ask why the Church should allow us, who had not given to the Church for years, to take from the Church now? We both felt twelve inches high.

*John:* We sat there with eyes as big as sewer lids and our jaws on the floor and we muttered, "Uhuh, uhuh," and made all the right noises, and we would occasionally look at each other out of the corner of our eyes every time he stopped to pat his damn dog. By then I had made up my mind that our wedding was going to be a civil ceremony. But suddenly he stopped his speech, felt inside his desk, and whipped out forms. He didn't ask us whether we agreed to any of what he said. He merely said, "Here are the forms—you fill them out. This is your M1." At which point I was so giddy from what had happened that I said, "Oh, you mean the money supply," and he said "What?" I explained, "In American financial circles the amount of money which is circulating at any one given moment is called the M1—the money supply." And he looked at me without humour and proceeded to instruct us on filling out the form. He said, "What day were you thinking of? Oh yes, there's an opening there." From his speech I suppose he thought he had got us to agree to the following: a) to go to Mass every Sunday, from now on for ever, and b) to go to an Engaged Encounter weekend. No ifs, ands, or buts. My impression of all this was a bit like a quota system. It was important for the right number of bodies to be carted into the Engaged Encounter weekend!

*Lyn:* We had to swear on the Bible before we filled out the forms. There were two separate forms, with questions like, Where do you live? Have you been married before? There were also questions about contraception, and Father Robinson took great pains to explain that we need not approach that question literally, and allowed that the Church realizes that some Catholics do practise birth control. We each then had to go through a one-on-one form-filling with him which had us totally terrified, because we were sure the other person would say something that might betray us. It was like an oral exam. But we passed the test and we had the date. I had to find out about the Engaged Encounter we had agreed to attend, so I called up and they were booked solid for months. We wound up with a weekend a month before our wedding date and they kept telling us how lucky we were to get in.

*John:* To be honest, I was disappointed to hear that they had an opening at all as we were already having visions of an Est type of confrontation. We had read an article in a magazine on the Catholic Church today, and set out in a sidebar was an exposé of some of the more extreme measures the right wing of the Catholic Church espoused, along with a statement that the Archdiocese of Montreal had deemed Engaged Encounter to be psychologically and physically abusive.

Of course we got very upset before the weekend. We had all sorts of contingency plans—at what point we would get up and walk out, whether we would sacrifice the whole chapel business, the wedding date, how far we were going to push it. But it was in for a dime, in for a dollar at this point.

*Lyn:* We realized now that we were playing a game and that we had to keep playing it. But as time went on, more and more horrors were revealed to us.

*John:* We paid our money for the weekend, which took place in an old nunnery in Quebec's Eastern Townships. We told our friends we were off to the Catholic Est, which is literally what it turned out to be. We arrived to find wretched sleeping accommodations. (You had to bring a sleeping bag and a snack for the communal table. You were given a checklist—just like going off to summer camp.) We were surrounded by very young, very sincere-looking people.

*Lyn:* We were the oldest people there—by ten years, at least. The whole principle of the weekend was to "communicate". Ironically, they were probably not aware that John and I were professional communicators—being writers. Anyway, we came in and everyone was sitting in a circle. There were two couples who were leading the seminar—one a very young couple who had been married a short period of time and the other an older couple who had been married for quite a long time and had children—and there in the midst was a priest. We were given some explanation of the weekend and the first exercise was that we all had to go around and explain what it was about the other person that had made us fall in love with them. There were comments like "She had such a great personality" or "such a good sense of humour"; "What attracted me to him was that he was so stable, so good-looking"—all the cliché things, and when my turn came I was totally unprepared for it, and I said, "I am marrying him because he is the best journalist in the city," and John said, "I am marrying her because she is the best novelist in the city," and of course nobody knew how to respond to this! Though in fact it proved to us that the relationship started on the basis of professional respect. Each of us was then handed a notebook and a pen and we were given thirteen topics to discuss—such as "Communication", "Christ in marriage", "The sacrament of marriage", "How to resolve fights". The priest gave a talk about his experience on these matters *vis-à-vis* the Church—which was his spouse—and then each couple had to read from the great big black folders we had been given which we knew were scripts written especially for them. We were then segregated—boys to one end of the room, girls to the other (not men and women, note)—and required to write answers on each of the topics. We had twenty minutes by ourselves, and then came back for twenty minutes together—hand each other our notes and discuss how our answers differed so that we might find some common ground to solve all these problems that we might have between us. It reminded me of charades.

*John:* For instance you would have questions like "How do you regard sex and marriage?" and we'd answer "Yes". Of course we got through them in about seven minutes and we sat for the rest of the time waving at each other, while the other couples were writing out long, long answers.

*Lyn:* A lot of the exercises were formed with the notion that "Now you have decided to get married you must discuss these things." Of course John and I had discussed them well before we decided to marry. The whole thing was ludicrous. It reminded us of cult retreats—or what we hear about them. It had a sort of Moonies feel to it. The first night was made up of opening chats by the couples and the priest. We were surrounded by tacky banners saying, "One by one we go into marriage," and "God is love." However, right before we retired the priest gave a short, sharp lecture on some couples not taking it seriously. So we went off to our separate beds. The following day was the same—totally regimented—priest talks, couples doing their thing—new pieces of paper given—off to write—come back, confer etc.

*John:* Because we got through the stuff in five minutes we started doing jokes. Mainly to keep ourselves amused through the monotonous stupid procedure.

*Lyn:* At this point John and I began to consider some of our contingency plans. But we knew that Father Robinson had to have the bit of paper saying we had completed the Encounter or he would blow the whistle on the whole thing, and we were only a month away from the day.

I was sharing my bedroom with an Anglican who was marrying a devout Quebec Catholic who was in the army. They were both in their early twenties. She was also going through conversion. I mentioned that the priest was obviously referring to John and me when he scolded us and she just laughed and said it was probably written into the script. It took an Anglican to be aware of the manipulation.


*John:* The whole weekend was scripted. The Moonies couldn't have done it better! On the Saturday night, we had a sixties-type rap session—mattresses pulled out on the floor, sacristy candles lit up in heart shapes along the floor—all the lights off. The idea was that under the cover of darkness we could say what was truly on our minds about marriage. Also, if at any time of day anyone had any questions, they could write them down and put them into a shoe box— the questions were then drawn out at random and discussed anonymously. The most common questions, of course, were about contraception, but the priest said, "We won't discuss it. It would require six months in a course of theological rudiments and there's no time now." All the girls were sitting back—you could feel the tension in the air, because they didn't want babies right away. I felt the rage in the room when he refused to discuss it.

*Lyn:* The irony of it all was that by the end of the entire process Father Robinson's dire warning had come true—we were prostituting the Church. We had started off not wanting to and they had forced us into doing so by throwing up rules and regulations which we couldn't question or, worse still, were not allowed to question, and we just toed the line, getting angrier and angrier.

*John:* But when the time came for the wedding, I was moved by the ceremony and by the words. Father Lowry managed to imbue the ritual with meaning, which is what we wanted—a way of publicly committing ourselves in front of our friends and families; it was a sacrament.

*Lyn:* Although we didn't have a Mass. Father Lowry said, "Well, you won't want a Mass," realizing what we had been through. He unilaterally decided not to put us through confession, so we didn't receive communion at our wedding. He didn't even ask—he just decided, and that was fine, I was so exhausted by the process. I was grateful for what we got in the end. We wanted God to bless the union, but we were not willing to jump through any more hoops. The Eucharist was not that important to me after we had gone through this whole rigmarole.

On reading again through John and Lyn's transcript, and listening to their voices on my tape recorder, I fully share their emotions. I share their anger and despair at the stupidity of the Church. I share their frustration while seeking an intelligent priest. I feel their sadness as they were forced to come to terms with a Catholicism that was obviously not the Catholicism of their youth. They were forced to accept that there was no turning back, while not being shown the way forward. They were at a standstill. But who was to blame?

I'm afraid John and Lyn were as guilty as the Catholic diocese and clergy in their town. They are enquiring intellectuals. But they showed little intelligence in the way they approached the Catholic Church when they decided to try to pick up the pieces of their Catholicism. They had lost touch with their religion; they had not kept abreast of the developments and changes that had taken place in the contemporary Church, and they were also unaware of the limitations put on clergy by a powerful right-wing diocese.

They favoured Father Lowry's liberal line but they made the mistake of thinking that he individually had the power to make their marriage happen outside the normal channels. If they had taken the care and the time to understand the makeup of a diocese, they would have found that, under Canon Law, this was unlikely. And in the end their friend Father Lowry deprived them, perhaps unintentionally, of the sacred carrot at the end of the whole episode, the Eucharist at their wedding. How could they be Catholic when deprived of the very Catholic symbol itself, the body of Christ?

So Lyn and John got married in a chapel they adored with a priest who did not blurt out right-wing rhetoric, with lilies on the altar and friends and family around. No Mass, no communion. A Christian marriage, yes, but not a Catholic one, which is what they had intended and were entitled to. They went through all that painful preparation for naught. It would have been easier for them to have married in a Protestant church. There they would have received communion without a fuss. But it wasn't the same clubhouse, the same tradition, it wasn't the same as being Catholic.

Many Catholics who have drifted away from the Church consider returning because of their desire for the Sacraments. And because, in a number of cases, they have been absent from Catholic practice for so long, the procedure becomes quite emotional for them. In a way, they view it as a return to their homeland, with all the understandable feelings of nostalgia.

John and Lyn had been rebels and drifters during their twenties; they "went travelling", like most people, and they came back to find their own country not quite the same as when they left. And they felt displaced, let down and angry, that the place wasn't what they expected and that no member of the clergy rushed out to hug them and welcome them back. They forgot that in their travels they had experienced new things, and had matured and become adults.

John and Lyn obviously felt they were entitled to a welcome like that received by the Prodigal Son. But the true meaning of the parable—of forgiveness and celebration, of prodigal regret, remorse of conscience, abject apology, and reformation—was absent on both sides. Their mistake was that they looked to members of the clergy to be without fault or human foolishness, to provide unquestioning sympathy and understanding for their reasons for being away. They thought priests were like the father in the parable, who celebrates the lost son who returns home by offering him the same rights and love he has shown to the brother who has been loyal and has remained labouring, without complaint, on the family farm. They took the Church for granted. They found out, unfortunately, that the Catholic Church does not "make merry and be glad" for the lost brother who "was dead and is alive", "was lost and is found". Their room was not kept for them with its sweet smells of incense, its flickering candles, its smiling statues, and its friendly tunes.

It seems to me that Lyn and John's decision to have a Catholic marriage should have been only the start of their religious renewal. Instead, the experience they underwent has pushed them further away from Catholic practice. Today, when I meet them, they openly admit they have "had it" with Catholicism. But we always find time to discuss its complexities—it intrigues them to know that I can still find so much in it to interest me. They now have a baby who has not been properly baptized. They didn't wish to repeat any of what they had gone through to get married, so instead they appointed a Catholic godfather—who is reported to have quietly baptized her himself one afternoon, over the kitchen sink.

There is no doubt that intelligent discernment and commitment are vital among members of the clergy. Yet the church's makeup, its business side—the organization of ceremonies, procedure, and preparation—is, in many urban centres, like a bureaucracy. You fill in forms and wait your turn. Because Lyn and John were unaware of the procedures of this bureaucracy before they stepped into it, they had no idea how to escape later on and demand some individual attention. They had got over the first hurdle, of finding a priest they liked and respected, but they did not know how to go a step further in their quest for renewal and understanding. But the question that springs to my mind is, where is Father Lowry now? Could he not have understood their dilemma, and visited them later, talked to them, invited them to church occasionally, got to know their daughter?

John and Lyn's experience in the Engaged Encounter was undoubtedly abysmal. But it is the song, not the singer, that counts, and, as in any large organization, moments of stupidity can easily be countered with informed common sense.

I am reminded of the story of a French couple living in Toronto, Lorraine and Pierre. Pierre hardly ever went to church, but Lorraine attended Mass on average about twice a month. When their first child, a son, was born, they met with the parish priest to arrange his baptism. The priest told them that first they had to attend the pre-baptism course for parents. Pierre, not a man to be pushed around, stood up immediately and said sternly, "I am a Catholic and my wife and I were married in the Church." He told the priest that his son was automatically entitled to baptism, and that he wasn't going to the course. He even threatened to go to another parish if his demands were not met. The calendar was then quickly pulled from the wall and the date confirmed. The course was never mentioned again.

Though the Church is essentially a spiritual institution, it is also a large and complex hierarchy sprawled over the centuries and around the globe. As such it has, inevitably, a massive bureaucracy. It is up to the individual Catholic to distinguish between personal faith and the rules and regulations surrounding it, and to have the confidence and determination to battle through. Rediscovering Catholicism (even staying in shape as a Catholic) requires a willingness to fight—to fight for one's personal faith, and to fight for equality within the Roman Catholic Church.

# 9

# THE PRIESTFORCE

"Today we need inspiring intellectual-spiritual
authority on all levels. But in many dioceses we
have merely clerical officials with more of a Roman
than of a Catholic mentality."

— HANS KÜNG, *What Must Remain in the
Church*

When Pope John Paul II visited Canada, I was one of a few
writers asked to prepare a short piece on him for a magazine,
not as the pontiff, the Bishop of Rome, or Primate of Italy, but
just as a person. I was in stimulating company. The editor of the
magazine had carefully selected from a variety of Catholics and
non-Catholics, and I noticed, when reading their commentaries,
that it was the non-Catholics who saw the Pope the way we
should all view him: as a diplomat and a monarch and, because
of his artistic streak, also as a poet—although the reviewer of his
poems, a fiery Jewish poet, found them uninspiring and lacking
in passion; to him they read like "notes for possible sermons"
and "praiseworthy feelings that might get some troubled priest
or nun through a difficult night." However, even if this Pope
could not be exalted to the company of Wordsworth or Blake,
his stylishness of dress and manner impressed another writer, an
artist who commented that his "public appearances rival those of
royalty in their pomp and circumstance." A theologian likened
the Pope to a "cheerful uncle from Europe", and one woman
wrote that just the experience of his presence had a lasting effect:
"People are better to one another and more socially concerned
after the Pope passes through."

There existed among the contributors who were not Catholic a kind of non-denominational reverence and respect for the Pope which was not readily shared by my Catholic friends. The latter complained about how much the whole thing cost, and thought the money would have been better spent to help the needy of the world. They did not welcome the rockstar-like adulation, the parades through the streets on today's version of the donkey, the Popemobile, nor the interminable touching of hands and kissing of children along the way. No, for them the Pope's visit just opened up all the old wounds. They dreaded him making retrograde remarks about the usual social sins, and presenting the Church as regressive, right-wing, and out of touch with their world. They pointed out that they felt no hostility for the Pope himself, only for what he stood for as the authoritative and powerful head of a very rich bureaucratic organization. Their dread was probably also triggered by all the past reverential fears of childhood which come to the fore at the mention of the "Holy Father", or the "Vicar of Christ".

Because so much of what is said and published today by the Pope and the Vatican does not jibe with what most Catholics believe to be Christ's original message of love, humility, and forgiveness, the pomp of a papal tour seems to many like an open display of heresy. One can see how easy it is to think this, because the practices and messages from the institutional Church are and always have been delivered in the name of the Lord, according to Paul's instructions in his Letter to the Colossians (3:17):

> And whatever you do, in word or deed, do everything
> in the name of the Lord Jesus, giving thanks to God
> the Father through him.

Generally we perceive the Vatican as a religious collective of holy men, with the Pope as listening post for God and—

like Moses before him—His interpreter. Whatever their personal opinions, most Catholics do have a reverence and respect for the papacy, and some welcome the conviction with which it promotes its teachings. As actress Elizabeth puts it, the Pope is a great public relations figure—"The Catholic Church has finally got a visible spokesman," she says, "even if he is incredibly rigid."

But I believe that we should not take the papacy as it is given. We should instead stand back and try looking at it from different perspectives, to see how the Pope and the Church could fit into another place in our lives.

In Chapter One I mentioned how Catholics sometimes misinterpret the meaning of "the Church", believing only in the institutional body and not contemplating the idea of a looser community of people with common Christian interests, and interpret "the faith" as being the code of Catholic existence when in fact it is a collection of Vatican-manufactured instructions for the religious robot. What is left, then, for the individual Catholic? Only what God gave us to begin with—a conscience and a soul, and the indefinable personal feelings and religious beliefs of the individual: what can be called, simply, "faith". "The faith" and "faith" are separate states—one public and the other private, one the Vatican and the other you; recognizing the division between the two gives us some perspective on the complexities of Catholicism.

The next thing to consider is, can we live as Catholics possessing only one part and ignoring the other? And can we, as free-thinking ordinary human beings, survive in isolation without a foundation of discipline and an active sense of belonging to history? I do not believe so. But I do believe that we are limited in our capacity to interpret religious symbols as they have been handed down through time, as well as to recognize how they relate to our everyday life. This is one reason we find it difficult to see how the institutional Church can have anything to do with us. Tess, the doctor from Ireland, told me, "I just can't abide some of the attitudes of the Vatican. I think anybody who thinks couldn't." But even as thinkers we are inclined to misinterpret the Church's efforts at symbolic interpretation. Of course, mis-interpretation is and always has been the most common source of frustration for members of the human race. As the Ameri-can moralist David Mall says, "The very words we choose to express a behavioral commitment toward others help make that commitment appear good or bad, desirable or undesirable." And Catholic dogma is no exception.

The Catholic problem is not unlike that of translators at a meeting of the United Nations, where the leaders of the world debate and decide on economic and political strategy through an impractical garble of wires and earphones. Yet the individuality of language, being a means of historic identity, keeps nationality alive and united while at the same time distinguishing it— as Latin perhaps once set apart and united Roman Catholics everywhere. Latin was the universal language of prayer, and since its general abolition many Catholics have understandably suffered identity crises and a sense of loss. Even if the meaning of every word or every sentence was not specifically understood, Latin added a dimension of spirituality and mystery to Catholic worship as well as a sense of historical and classical significance. I know that for me not understanding every word of an opera adds magic to the performance, as the recital of the sixteenth-century Tridentine Mass once did. It is not fashionable any more *not* to understand each other, not to be unified. But in translation there is a danger that the message may be watered down and simplified. There is some reason to mourn the fact that we are expected now to simplify everything to the $n$th degree, instead of employing images or metaphors that may be unclear to some.

However, symbolism helps us to grasp that other means of communication, the most mysterious—that which exists without form. Communication without language is and always has been the most powerful—not only in prayer to God, but also between people. We discover this in sexual expression and in simple communion with nature. Our need and hunger for this essential language belongs to the soul, as it is free, unrestricted, and therefore not wholly of this world. It was made manifest in the purest way when the Apostles, gathered together in a room, were touched by the Holy Spirit so that they spoke in many tongues, which surely is—in the metaphorical spirit of the New Testament—the wordless conversation where all meaning is understood, the language all mortals desire and don't succeed in obtaining until, perhaps, the next life.

Some of us do manage to get glimpses of what has been before, or is to come, in this life, and this confirms the many hidden powers we have to communicate on a higher plane. The soul and the conscience seem connected in this area—being a part of our spiritual makeup. Our spiritual attributes can be separate entities and yet, at the same time, a part of the one. This is not unlike the idea of the one God as three—the Father, the Son, and the Holy Spirit. Each of the Catholics I interviewed had a different personal sense of God—some pray to the Father, some to the Son and the Spirit (and saints and mortals and Mary)—but this does not mean that personal preference is exclusive. No Catholic would need to revoke God the Father because he or she prefers to pray to God the Son, or would even think in terms of "faith" without "hope" and "charity", or "charity" without "hope" and "faith". So why is it not possible to think this way about Catholicism? If the ideas and inspirations we receive from religious metaphor can go beyond the dictates of the Church—if "faith" and "the faith" can be separate states—why do so many Catholics believe they must be solely one and the same? After all is said and done, it is still very hard for people to comprehend a whole as being divisible.

Catholicism as one symbolic whole is divisible, composed of a variety of symbolic parts. If we took to viewing it as separate parts, placing those parts in their proper perspective as they affect our own beliefs and needs, then it would be a lot easier to accept the presence of the Pope and the Vatican in our daily lives. It is up to the individual Catholic alone to decide on their place—side by side with private faith, or behind it, before it, or slightly above it. The Catholic institution will never go away, never disappear altogether, because the Catholic Church is very much a part of not only our spiritual world but our secular world as well.

## The Kingdom of This World

There are some cities I have visited that I believe are not completely of this world. I don't mean manufactured kingdoms like Disneyland, with its Sleeping Beauties and snapping dragons, but real places of human spirit—noisy, smelly cities of motion—Athens, Venice, New York. I pick these three because I know them and have spent much time in them alone, wandering and observing. But I choose them for another reason too: they are examples of perfection and imperfection, ugliness and beauty, in juxtaposition; they mirror the extremes of human toil; they are symbols of what we are in our Original Sin. I remember standing on the hill of the Acropolis while the wind blew across the sky of deep blue and the wide expanse of rubble—the ancient stones, the pillars of power, were like personalities from another age, winking from every corner, and as I looked down on the great stinking metropolis of twentieth-century Athens, and heard its car horns, I noticed a filthy cloak of pollution wrapping itself around the base of the temples. I thought then of how it would be if there were no sin, no greed, no noise, no pollution, and realized that there'd be nothing but old stones, a few farm animals, and a smattering of lifeless shacks. Without war there would have been no Acropolis; without sin, no saints. A boring world, a world no human could exist in. And suddenly I wanted desperately to be an observer no longer, but to get down into the noise and partake of it all, like the ant perhaps.

New York has the same effect on me: the island of Manhattan—a place where the rich and poor live side by side, a place to pursue artistic and architectural perfection, a place of ghettos for the different races, freedom for the individual, oppression of space and time. A city, if you view it from the water or the air, that is certainly not of this world but something from another planet, something of the future, a shining example of what we've become.

The Italian writer Italo Calvino created places of his imagination around the idea of Venice, where paradise existed within a landscape of evil and descent. Venice, the backdrop of our mediaeval past, sinking slowly into the muddy, smelly swamp, wrapped in a pink mist.

And then there is Vatican City. Why should anyone believe it is the only city immune to the world? If you look in on the smallest kingdom you will marvel at its outward perfection. It's just over a hundred acres in size, yet it has such powerful resources that it can remain totally independent—like the Venice of yesteryear. Its citizens jostle about their daily duties, some dressed in costumes of the carnival, a colourful array of black and white and purple, red and yellow. They live amid the great buildings around their cathedral—the museums, libraries, colleges, and palaces. There's a radio station, a printing press (for stamps and the daily newspaper), a helicopter port, a fire station, quite a few gardens, and there are even law courts and a power plant. But in this fairytale land where the birds sing, the bread is freshly baked, and the cabbages grow, corruption stirs in the dark corners and alleyways, like an old blind white snake.

A bird's eye view of Vatican City reveals little to differentiate it from the rest of Rome. It looks a part of the bustling megalopolis, a city which was there long before it was. However, it is unique in that it has managed to separate itself legislatively and become a city within a city. If we stop *looking* and start *thinking* about this, in symbolic terms, then Vatican City becomes what we imagined it to be—a city on a mountaintop, a Shangri-La where sin does not exist.

It would be healthier for Catholics to look at the institutional Church the way a nation does its monarchy. Being British by birth and Catholic by baptism, I often liken my feeling towards the papacy and the Vatican to those I feel for the Queen and the Royal Family—a reverent indifference. My feelings are not unusual. Many British people find even the idea of the monarchy distasteful—an institution that propagates an elitist environment within a society built on class bias. But others welcome this fairytale as a symbol of continuity, of stability and the strength of tradition, and as a reminder that life's not all misery and hardship, and that there's something to be proud of. In England, as in most old countries, there are castles, gardens, and majestic fountains; there are old family estates packed full of paintings and murals; there are cathedrals, chapels, and libraries full of books and scripts; there is music, from coronation marches to requiems for the dead; there is the ritual and the heraldry, the arms and armouries, the ships that sailed the world bearing royal insignias and celebrating the strength and courage of a nation of united peoples. Similarly, Catholics all over the world, whatever their own country's political state, have the glory of the Catholic nation, and can be caught up in wonder and awe over their own particular heritage—the glorious places of worship, the exceptional paintings, the music and artistry, and other evidence of man's celebration of God. It is easy to forget the fat stock investments, land claims, and cash trades which are the material power of the Vatican. And many Catholics are unaware that the church does not pay taxes. To most, Vatican City is still a saintly kingdom. Such thinking carries with it all the ignorance of a child.

The Vatican, though, is no longer as mysterious and inaccessible as it once was. The Pope is constantly travelling around

140

the world, with the attendant media revealing him as an accessible, touchable human being; a number of popular books, and many magazine pieces, have opened the doors of the Vatican to general view. Yet, while we are allowed to look in, this does not necessarily mean that Rome will look out.

It is imperative for Catholic people to speak out, through the sophisticated electronic media, about their dissatisfaction with Rome's unyielding stubbornness over contemporary issues. If this does not take place on an ongoing basis the Pope, and many of the cardinals and bishops, will continue in their present way, conducting their business in the name of the Lord, as always, but with little sympathy for the people; and we will have contributed, in our complacency, to helping the Catholic Church remain where it wants to be—in a superior position to ourselves.

## *Gaining a Balance of Power*

For the Catholic Church to grow, and for individual Catholics to believe that they are part of the Church, equality must exist. The ideal balance of power between the institutional Church and the laity would obviously be one of equal weight. In illustration it might look something like this:

| The Kingdom of This World | The Kingdom Not of This World |
|---|---|
| Vatican-Affiliated Institution | The Person and God |
| "The Faith" | "Faith" |

How can a healthy balance between Catholics and Catholicism be gained? How can the Vatican become a more equal partner? The answer lies in understanding—in "thinking, testing, and searching" as my mother's lay Catholic group once wrote in a letter to their bishop. But such understanding can only be achieved by a course of personal education—and one might first investigate how the present structure is set up, and become aware of the makeup of the central power and workings of the institutional Church, before exploring ways and means of achieving personal equality within the system.

First we need to recognize two key points:

1) *That the Church is not infallible:* The Church is an institution, not a vast spiritual body. Being misinformed about the way it is run, and who the players are, can only lead to personal disappointment, disillusionment, and religious confusion.

2) *That the Church is divisible:* The Church, however, is made up of a number of other churches—the spiritual, the secular, and the communal. The power that Rome holds in the world is largely due to its worldliness, but its spiritual power is mostly due to its citizens.

The chart illustrates the breakdown of the hierarchy of the institutional church, headquartered in Rome. If you looked at it with a purely secular eye, you might interpret it as a family tree, or a royal genealogical table, or perhaps, more appropriately, an organization chart of a multinational company. There's the Pope as chairman of the board in the company's headquarters in Rome, and around him are his vice-presidents— the cardinals (numbering approximately 160). Then there are his managing directors, the bishops and archbishops (of whom there are approximately 2,300), who are called to head office for the annual general meeting or any other crucial decision-making conferences. An example would be the October 1987 Synod of Bishops, for which the Pope called together about 220 bishops

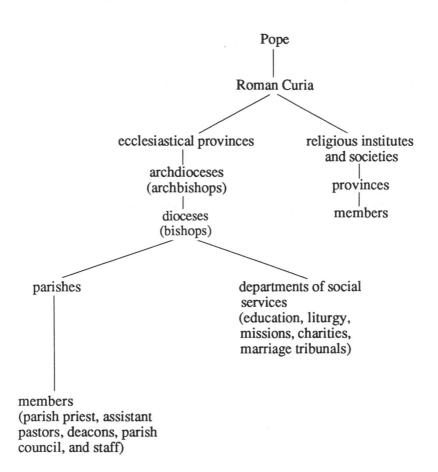

Pope
|
Roman Curia

ecclesiastical provinces       religious institutes
|                   and societies
archdioceses
(archbishops)       provinces
|
dioceses       members
(bishops)

parishes       departments of social
services
(education, liturgy,
missions, charities,
marriage tribunals)

members
(parish priest, assistant
pastors, deacons, parish
council, and staff)

from around the world to discuss, behind closed doors, the "vocation and mission of the laity in the Church and in the world twenty years after the Second Vatican Council"—a conference, in other words, on the future of the non-ordained lay people who make up 99 per cent of the Church's membership. The Pope presides over such conferences. The managing directors make their views known to the chairman, report to him what's going on in the divisions (their dioceses), and represent the interests of their branch managers, assistant managers, and co-ordinators— namely the parish priests, nuns, and curates. As in most well-run companies, the chairman of the board feels it is his responsibility to be aware of the needs of his company's customers out there in the real world, so the synods give him a further opportunity to keep a finger on the pulse of the consumers, in addition to his travels.

There is one weak link in this company's chain, however. It is not that the company is losing money (its assets are reported to be in the multi-billions), but that it has not recognized one of the most significant social (and corporate) concerns of the last decade: equal opportunity. Equality of the sexes has been rejected within the organization. Its policy towards the role of women workers in the company is somewhat archaic, and the idea of equality at a management level is totally unacceptable. The company's problem seems to be that it requires a theoretical argument that will support a definition of basic equality before it can even countenance the presence of women in roles of responsibility. Female members of the human race are accepted only within the structural moulds created for them by a male-run organization that operates within a biblical context that has barely changed in two thousand years.

The role models are as follows:

*The Virgin*, who is chaste and forever servile
*The Wife*, who looks after her husband

*The Mother*, who looks after her son
*The Whore*, who looks after men.

Saint Paul made clear on many occasions in the New Testament what he felt about the preferred state of female subordination. One managing director has plainly stated that the company does not look favourably on equality in management since a woman's place should still be very much in the home:

> The rationalized equality-as-identity removes marriage as the fundamental social structure, the intrinsic and indispensable realization of the equality-in-difference of men and women. It is through marriage that men and women accept and undertake their qualitatively different responsibilities. It is through marriage that men and women constitute their freedom in the community.
>
> "Do This in Memory of Me",
> Gerald Emmett Cardinal Carter

It is not hard to see how the idea of women in power might appear as a threat to the existing corporation as an international network of men. If women were promoted to positions of management, the same managing director said, the move would lead to "a community so conceived along rationalist lines that it possesses no inherent structure or feature by which it might be distinguished from any other secular community." Another excuse given is that no woman was seated at the Last Supper, and so women should not be included in the constitution of the Church. Clearly the issue is not the quality of contribution that women make, but simply the male collective's determination to protect the tradition of its past members as well as the activities of its present members, by not officially acknowledging that contribution through ordination and promotion. The company, so as not to avoid confusion or misinterpretation of its rules, has issued its own version of its official code in the Canon Law, which clearly outlines the status quo and defines the roles of the staff and the rules they are to work under.

Leadership of a company or a nation is usually a task one is trained for. So when a well-meaning cardinal is dropped into the bureaucratic hotbed of Vatican City—expected to lead it with all the estimable qualities of a chief executive officer or president, while maintaining the spiritual responsibility of representing Christ to the world—one can appreciate the huge task at hand. But the Holy See, in assuming the divine authority given the Pope, makes it easier for him by bestowing on him the power to personally veto anything within Catholic jurisdiction—and in many cases outside it too. This is written succinctly in the Canons:

> The office uniquely committed by the Lord to Peter, the first of the Apostles, and to be transmitted to his successors, abides in the Bishop of the Church of Rome. He is the head of the College of Bishops, the Vicar of Christ, and the Pastor of the universal Church here on earth. Consequently, by virtue of his office, he has supreme, full, immediate and universal ordinary power in the Church, and he can always freely exercise this power.
> Can. 331

> There is neither appeal nor recourse against a judgement or a decree of the Roman Pontiff.
> Can. 333, 3

This makes the Pope more powerful than any monarch, head of state, or chairman of a multinational company. But there are all sorts of ironies here. The Holy See has been likened

146

to the Politburo, a comparison evoked perhaps by the great, cumbersome bureaucratic machine over which it has command, by the secrecy of its operations, and by the tendency of the Vatican to interfere in the political arena. The Vatican, as an independent state, is represented in the United Nations and has a number of treaties and accords with countries, including some under Communist rule such as Yugoslavia, Cuba, and South Korea, as well as some Moslem countries actively involved in fighting Christian resurgence. In 1984 the United States re-established full diplomatic relations with the Vatican, after a breach of over a hundred years, citing its recognition of the large moral and political influence it has in the world and of the courageous stand the Pope has taken in defence of Western values. Yet it is the Vatican's political passivity which makes it a strong attraction in the secular world. With the absence of military strength, it wields its political power through its spiritual ties to most Catholics through its clergy.

The political supremacy of the Church grew over the centuries within Europe in much the same way that the Roman Empire had extended its influence before—its soldiers spreading the word by speech, by letter, and sometimes by the sword. And with the immigrant movements of Europeans to North America, it spread this power farther afield. It was after the end of the Second World War that there came a considerable shift in the power base. Today, the Catholic population of the Third World—Asia, Africa, and Latin America—outnumbers that of Europe and North America, bringing the Church's influence to bear on the political hotspots of the globe, where overcrowding, unemployment, poverty, and general daily strife lead regularly to violence and sometimes to revolution. Amid the turmoil, the Vatican, which advocates peaceful solutions to terrorist actions, warns against the clergy becoming openly affiliated with radical political factions. Priests who favour revolutions, as in Nicaragua, for instance, are removed to other parts of the country by their

bishops in an effort to combat this. The Pope sends his repre-
sentatives to visit imprisoned members of the IRA, and bishops
publish pastoral reports recommending social justice. The Pope's
role in the political arena is not so much that of spiritual leader
as of peacemaker. But it is becoming increasingly difficult for
him to remain neutral. The Vatican issues encyclicals advocat-
ing worker ownership of industries as labourers clock in to work
at Vatican City.

The Holy See and its bureaucracy make up not only a
business but a government, which has to confront the ethical
dilemmas that normally go hand in hand with corporate or
diplomatic power. There was the scandal surrounding a Vatican-
affiliated bank, which led to the suicide of its principal and to
suspicions about the business affairs of the Church, many of
which remain unresolved. There have been charges that free-
thinking clergy who advocate greater clerical autonomy are
silenced by tactics resembling those the Soviet Union employs
against dissidents: they are called back to the Vatican, and kept
there to do tasks under the ever-watchful eye of a bigger brother.
The German theologian Hans Küng has repeatedly pointed a
finger at Rome for crying out for human rights in the world while
neglecting them inside its own house.

But if the Vatican is not a celestial place, its government
not free from sin, its power not free from abuse, and its ranks not
without stain, how is it that we believe it to be holy and allow it
to maintain such a strong hold on our lives? Perhaps it is because
we misunderstand its true motives.

The makeup and structure of the Catholic constitution, and the
Church's methods of government, have not undergone any radical change in the last few centuries. It is only recently that the
idea of decentralizing the hierarchy has been broached by priests
and nuns favouring a freer hand within their own parishes and

orders, to let them consider their own local requirements as opposed to those of Rome. The Vatican has interpreted this as the emergence of a possible power shift from the boardroom to the branches, and the idea has caused a certain degree of consternation at head office, even though a pull towards equality at a grass-roots level should have been considered exciting and innovative, and a logical extension to Vatican II's promotion of secularity and a closer association with members of the Catholic community. We had already experienced welcome cosmetic changes—Rome's willingness to have people milling around the altar in their ordinary clothes, sitting on parish committees, handling chalices and, in many cases, even the Eucharist—and all Catholics I have spoken to favour these progressive activities. That, combined with the fact that priests now face us in the celebration of Mass instead of rudely doing everything with their backs to us, indicated that better communication and more open discourse were in store. But unfortunately the spiritual intelligence of the Holy See seems to have been too limited to understand that the power shift towards greater autonomy for priests and nuns could lead to religious maturity and renewal, and a more informal and more vital Church. Instead it fears the loss of central power and of the traditional way of operation. The renovations and more open concept promised by Vatican II remain half-finished; it seems as if the contractors have abandoned the job. Cracks are appearing in the stone floor. And instead of providing a new, sure foundation, the Vatican prefers to patch up the damage in the ancient stonework.

## Retrenchment

The first thing Rome attempted to do was to come up with new ways of enforcing conformity, and the obvious place to start was with members of the priestforce. If you look at the way in which Church rules are imposed as similar to the way in which secular laws are enforced, the Catholic cleric today could be classified as a police officer whose job is to serve the nation, keep law and order, and make sure the flock stays on the straight and narrow road of faithfulness.

In the past it was somewhat easier for the members of the priestforce to enforce regulations, since their uniforms were easily recognizable; particularly the female orders, who sported huge wimples or neat close-to-the-head bandages, large crucifixes around the neck, bibs in shades of blue and grey, and voluminous long skirts. Now it is not as fashionable to flaunt such eccentric attire, given the efforts made towards social integration between clergy and the laity. Nuns have exposed heads and legs, and priests may sport open-neck shirts and sweaters as an alternative to the more restricting white collar and black tunic. But however free the uniform—and whatever the motive for the new ease of clothing—members of the priestforce have never been allowed room to doubt their role as members of the institutional Catholic Church. The Holy See has clearly inscribed it for them in Canon Law. They must acknowledge that the supreme power lies with the pontiff, and then, in turn, with their own bishops under whom they serve in the dioceses:

> Clerics have a special obligation to show reverence and obedience to the Supreme Pontiff and to their own Ordinary.
>
> Can. 273

Their own power is restricted and minimal.

> Only clerics can obtain offices the exercise of which requires the power of order or the power of ecclesiastical governance. Unless excused by a lawful impediment, clerics are obliged to accept and faithfully fulfil the office committed to them by their Ordinary.
>
> Can. 274

They swear allegiance to their communities, which of course is essential if the collective Catholic community is to work at all. From here it is a small step to the idea of Christian brotherhood, which assists them in keeping to their vows of celibacy, is a reminder of their function as Christ's workers, and helps them into the larger group—the chaotic, misguided laity.

> Since all clerics are working for the same purpose, namely the building up of the body of Christ, they are to be united with one another in the bond of brotherhood and prayer. They are to seek to cooperate with one another, in accordance with the provisions of particular law.
>
> Can. 275, 1

So appointments of nuns and priests are made with Canon Law as the main reference. Preference is given not to individuals who show particular spiritual or theological ability, but to those who possess the quality of subservience and have no problem with integration into parish or convent or school life.

Anybody signing up for the priestforce today must be able to fit into the structure of Vatican conformity. The team needs good team members. The team cannot, understandably, accommodate independent thinkers or heroes.

In his 1982 paper "The Clergy, Secularization and Politics", David Martin of the London School of Economics points out that there has been a strong tendency for the role of the common priest to change from the academic of the past, the intellectual, sage, or professor who was very much a part of "work-centred culture", to the priest today who is more of an organizer of the day-to-day activities of the local priest station, a member of the "home-centred culture". He explains, too, that

The old individualistic, personalized approach has been eroded in many professions in favour of the collective exercise of a limited personal competence.

Given the demands and requirements of the Catholic Church today, there is a real danger that new recruits to the regular priestforce will be those who possess the qualities that will make them not active participants in the Church, in a loose-knit community of Christian people, but passive participants of Rome, the yes-men and yes-women of our society, the followers not of Christ but of the institutional Church, and the bowers and scrapers to its authority.

Such a situation encourages other problems. Nowadays the priestforce has become a holy alternative to the secular army for many a society outcast or social misfit. By just going through the motions of seminarian life, by following the rules and by not upsetting the status quo, a young recruit can be awarded a religious title, and can, with little effort, become a hero to his friends and relatives and to most people who come in contact with him.

One priest in his early forties, Father Lewis, commented on his formation work in Pennsylvania, training young men for the religious life. "We help them have an idea of living in a corporate life with a spiritual dimension—and to know who you are and whether you are comfortable within the order, and what its particular role is within the Church. It is interesting that most people who come have insecurities about how they gain recognition in life, and in our order one of the unwritten laws is that if anyone is like that you try to slowly show them the door so they don't stay. Unfortunately, that's hard to detect sometimes, as people are good at dissimulation. We have had ordained people in our order who left two years from ordination, and we were quite pleased to see them go. But in many cases we couldn't detect their true character and commitment prior to that time since the façade was so good, their game even better."

I asked him to expand on the "game". "The game is to get accepted—to find a place where they can say 'I belong,' mostly because they don't feel good about themselves. They haven't dealt with a number of basic issues. Many strive for perfection—you know, the types who wouldn't say 'shit' if it was in their mouth. How can they really be themselves under these circumstances?"

The sacred dog-collar becomes in itself a symbol of distinction; being called "priest", "father", "brother", or "Reverend" elevates the ordinary man to a position of authority which promotes feelings of self-worth and feeds the ego.

At a time when Rome is attempting to promote conformity to its laws, denying individual conscience in favour of a collective consciousness, a disturbing possibility begins to emerge—that we could become surrounded by soullessness among the clergy.

A dichotomy now exists between the institutional Church and its staff, and the spiritual Church and its laity, who are pushing for more openness and more dialogue. Therefore, at a time when it is vital that the Church attract and recruit appropriate men and women to the religious life, with the skills necessary to communicate, the wrong people are signing up—or no one is signing up at all.

## Looking for Father Right

We were brought up through our Catholic education to believe that qualities of innovativeness are what we want and expect from members of the priestforce, as Lyn and John did when they decided to get married in the Catholic Church.

In my family we have one priest whom we all love and respect, mainly because of his intelligence, his sense of humour, and his nonconformity. Even though he is elderly now and semi-retired, he regularly gets called upon out of desperation to perform priestly functions like marrying one of us, baptizing somebody's child, or simply offering advice in times of need. My earliest memory is of Father Hamilton barging into our kitchen after the Good Friday service; and while we were all attempting solemnness on this solemn day, he announced that Easter Sunday was going to be a special one in the parish as he was substituting ice-cream cones for the host at communion, and wanted to take our orders for flavours right away. He took out a notebook and we all thought he was serious. Granny, who could not tolerate the idea, grunted and said she would prefer to stay with the old way, as she slowly departed out to the hall and back to the safe shrine of her room. My father decided this was a priest worthy of a seat at our table and invited him to stay for dinner. An old schoolfriend of mine from England said the other day that her life had opened up on meeting this same priest while in her teens; "He introduced me to Teilhard de Chardin and China tea!" she exclaimed.

We may all ask where such idealists, such individualists, such free-thinking, intelligent members of the clergy are these days. We seek out the heroes who can disturb the status quo and shake the Church out of its rigidity, and we expect to find them within the confines of Canon Law. We need to remind ourselves again that the Church is really no different from a large corporation, where the idea of entrepreneurship is welcome only as it relates to the corporation, not necessarily to its customers. It is naive to believe in the Catholic line that theories and laws are there for our own good when they are really only applicable to the clergy. For example, it is stated:

> Clerics are always to do their utmost to foster among people peace and harmony based on justice.
>
> Can. 287, 1

154

and:

> Clerics are to acknowledge and promote the mission
> which the laity, each for his or her part, exercises in
> the Church and in the world.
>
> Can. 275, 2

It can even be debated that Canon Law is not applicable to the lay, as it is, in effect, not a secular law. But, like any law, it is still open to independent interpretation, and the society of the Catholic Church appoints canon lawyers to carry out this task. In lay terms this can be viewed as the ultimate irony, seeing that most canon lawyers are members of the priestforce, and are there not to interpret the law for the laity but to uphold the Church's judicial system. In an effort to broaden the message and make the law applicable to all Catholics, though, Pope Paul VI wrote to priests in his encyclical *Humanae Vitae*,

> You know, too, that it is of the utmost importance, for
> peace of consciences and for the unity of the Christian
> people, that in the field of morals as well as in that
> of dogma, all should attend to the magisterium of the
> Church, and all should speak the same language.

The questions regarding language emerge again. What language? The language of the laws of the Vatican? Latin? The unspoken language of love? Probably all three—a trinity of communication which Catholic clergy may have once possessed and should probably still strive for. But perhaps it is the language of Christ, the message He tried to get across over the dicta and dogma of His age—and He only became a hero by taking a stand *outside* the religious structure.

I was disappointed to discover that it was the great spiritual innovator Pope John XXIII who said, "Avoid everything

155

which savours of singularity"—but perhaps he meant that an independent leader is an ineffective hero without followers and subordinates. Theorists would often be wasting their energy in the promotion of their ideas if they could not find ways of putting their theories into practice, slipping them easily into the already existing framework.

There are two types of heroes—the conforming and the nonconforming. The Church, given its structure, most easily houses the conforming hero, because the nonconforming hero is one whose visionary talents and independent skills have made him or her stand out in a crowd. The nonconformists are driven by a need to be different, to excel at what they do, to extend themselves to extreme physical and emotional degrees, not necessarily reaping rewards for themselves in this life. They are quite frequently disturbers of the status quo, like Christ Himself. Like Him, there have been many who died young. D.H. Lawrence, Yeats, and Orwell automatically spring to mind, and contemporary folk heroes like John Lennon. Many writers and artists have striven to understand humanity, and have tolerated personal isolation as a result of their nonconformity, their distaste for fitting in. They are, as the writer Graham Greene once described himself, like the grain of sand in the machine. But if we search for clergy with nonconforming qualities within the Catholic Church today we will be disappointed. "You see," said a bishop in London, "being a priest today requires walking a great tightrope between mission and maintenance." A job for the conforming hero, the person whose spiritual task and commitment are not lost in parish maintenance and politics.

This cleric would have to have the wisdom to recognize the need for material maintenance, to contribute to it without losing sight of the larger role he or she would have to play in practising as well as preaching the Gospel. The list of requirements for a priest today would include: an ability to organize, the maturity to handle the pressures of being everything to everyone, the capacity for delivering sermons of intelligence and understanding through a knowledge of scripture, superior qualities of oratory, compassion and patience and a sound grasp of psychology for effective counselling both in and out of the confessional, coming to terms with celibacy and the single life, an understanding of tradition yet an openness to ecumenicity, a capacity for secular thought within spiritual dimensions, a retention of personal values within the straitjacket of the Catholic constitution, a sense of humour, foresight, a non-sexist intelligence in speech and action, an apolitical stance within a political organization, and the ability to keep sight of the original message of Christ, which can vanish within the complexities of Canon Law and diocesan dogma. But the age when career decisions are usually made, just out of university or school, is not a time when such qualities are evident. Not until someone begins to handle the job do most of these abilities become clear. And for any human it is tough to retain a balance of commitment to the order, the diocese, Rome, God, the people, and celibacy, and still be able to "give out" constantly. However, while researching this book I did come across a few members of the priestforce in their mid-thirties to early forties who seemed to me to share conforming heroic qualities. They had the maturity to understand what and whom they were dealing with within the confines of the Church.

Father Andrew from Boston was one. He said, "I have begun to be very comfortable with who I am—recognizing my limitations but laying them on the table. I don't play games as I used to. I used to play games to look more holy, look better than I was—putting on appearances—now I know I am just a basic guy. If I have something to say, I say it. I try to preface everything by saying 'This isn't personal, but here I am.' The tenor of the Church and the tenor of the times make it easier for me to be me now because people accept the priest as human, whereas twenty to thirty years ago that wasn't the case. So I don't have to be all things to all people. I think that would be a tremendous pressure to live under. I don't know if I could have continued ordained had that been the case.

"But I have at times given off an air of self-righteousness, because I felt things had to change. This was in the initial year or two of my priesthood—of thinking, well, I must get in here and do something. I was fortunate that a lot of my peers spoke of this issue when we were going through seminary training— we were told that we were not going to change the world. We were told it was good to have ideals but they must be based on something—don't become complacent but don't lay that trip on others who are struggling in their own lives—priests, parishioners, or whoever. I may have offended people, though, as on the way I had this gung-ho idealism—I may have pushed them into thinking, 'Who is this snot?' 'Who does he think he is?' 'What does he know of life?' "

We talked about the problems inherent in the recruitment procedure as well as the qualities necessary to make ministry worth while.

"Well, of course, it's more than just intelligence, though I believe that's important—it's a basic security of self.... The hierarchical system in the Church develops the insecure, of course—the yes Monsignor, no Monsignor, whatever-moves-kiss-it Monsignor—because it's the only way to survive for a lot of people."

He then went on to tell me a story of a friend of his who was devout, bright, and committed to his future life as a minister (he was entering the priesthood at the mature age of forty). He patiently tolerated the kindergarten-like atmosphere of the seminary, which included a 10 p.m. curfew and, in an effort to stamp out suspected homosexuality, a ban on visits to the toilets after 11 p.m.

"Most of his colleagues were young, underdeveloped, im-mature, and few at that age would have the stamina and grace, as he did, to work through the nonsensical rules and see beyond. A lot of what is taught to seminarians, now anyway, is watered-down theology. Many who now hold responsible positions in parishes probably shouldn't—and a lot of people who are ordained should probably be taking further lessons in sound theology. There is a growing tendency towards ignorance in theological education, because Rome has laid down that no *former* priest or nun who has a diploma can teach theology in seminaries, nor can they teach in graduate classes and Master of Divinity courses in schools. They're the ones who could contribute so much! Everyone rules from fear. Even the seminaries can't grant degrees if they don't get diocesan approval."

Father Lewis from Pennsylvania commented that if there is no proper discrimination at the level of ordination it is "highly probable" that a growing number of Catholic people will be hurt or insulted.

"I know of many new priests," he said, "who think that now that they have fulfilled their obligations in becoming a minister all they have to do is carry out the duties and programs given to them and convey this information to the people. They don't seem to recognize that there must be human interaction and involvement with their communities. It is not only a matter of what is spoken but how it is spoken; people in positions of Church leadership have a role to play but it is not necessarily one of running to the supreme court, more an open dialogue and *contact.*"

This is a suitable place to share a recent incident I experienced when I dropped into Sunday evening Mass at the cathedral in Toronto's busy city centre. The congregation was made up of prominent middle-class people—there were more than two Mercedes parked outside the gates, and a profusion of sable and scent hung around the pews. On my left was a woman in her late twenties, clad in boots and a duffel coat. Her Sony Walkman was lying by her side as she leafed through the hymnal. We'd been through the Gospel reading of Mark 1:21–28, in which Christ gathers the first of his Apostles and goes into the synagogue at Capernaum to teach. We'd heard about the man who was obviously possessed by an unclean spirit, who cries out:

> "What have you to do with us, Jesus of Nazareth? Have you come to destroy us? I know who you are, the Holy One of God." But Jesus rebuked him, saying, "Be silent, and come out of him!" And the unclean spirit, convulsing him and crying with a loud voice, came out of him.

In this cathedral there is always a partitioning of roles. The older priests say Mass, and the young pastors deliver the rhetoric— if they are not reading from long, tedious pastoral letters. This time a young priest, not much older than twenty-five, climbed up to the podium. Short in stature, he pushed his face into the microphone so that he could be heard hurling his grenade into the congregation before him. This was his Homily.

(Cough.) "Today I want to make clear the church's teachings on masturbation, pre-marital sex, artificial birth control, and abortion." My neighbour squirmed in her seat, and there was a flutter of light coughing around me. "They are all very serious sins," Father Impudence went on. "I know that it is fashionable to believe that your conscience can determine what is a sin and what is not a sin, and I want to put the record straight right now. The Church has the wisdom to know what is best and I try and instil this when talking to people who come to me for marriage preparation. I constantly ask myself why people cannot see for themselves how damaging masturbation, pre-marital sex, and artificial birth control can be, and how beautiful sexual abstention is in the pursuit of the love of God. All these acts are grave sins and, like it or not, unless you confess them you are automatically excommunicated from the Church, because of the abuse

160

you have shown towards her, and in some cases for the mortal sin you have committed. Like abortion, for instance. It is all very well calling yourself a Catholic. It is a lie."

His voice rose. It was a squeaky one and he was shouting. I noticed that someone was steadily kicking the back of my pew, and I looked longingly at the Walkman as a way to eliminate the sound of his voice. I glanced around me and noticed the looks of disbelief on the faces of the furry people, and some of us eyed each other in sympathy, while Young Impy clattered on.

"You are only a member of the Catholic Church if you abide by the rules of the Catholic Church, and if when you do not you go to confession."

At this point I thought of leaving—walking out noisily, banging doors—and I wondered if others would accompany me. I was finding it hard to believe this was really happening, and I pinched my arm, not to waken myself from the nightmare but so I could survive this diatribe by making the emotional pain less significant. I then turned to prayer. I said to God, I will not let this whippersnapper ruin my Mass, I will not let his spittle make me so angry that I avoid going to communion out of hate; and I asked for strength to control myself. I have, evidently like all those around me, a reverence for holy places, and this stopped me from getting up and walking out or even getting up and shouting back. Father Imp knew this and was taking advantage of us all. He was even beginning to smile while he carried on. I was pleased to notice that the older priest in his chair was as embarrassed as we were. His ears had gone quite purple.

It was finally over and the older priest rose, took a deep breath (we heard it over the sound system), and muttered, virtually inaudibly, "Let us pray." But no one was praying, everyone was stunned.

After Mass, I sat and waited for the people to leave the church (many probably never to come back), because I had decided to have a talk with this priest. He was at the back of

161

the church shaking hands with the parishioners. I noticed that some even kissed him on the cheek (mostly people with large collections of noisy children), and I overheard from an older man, who had just counted out the collection and put the coins in velvet bags, "That was marvellous, Father—to have the courage to say what you did. About time too...." And all the while our Father Impudence was smiling, kissing, nodding, and shaking hands, unaware that I was about to hit him. I leaned against the holy water font, my anger deep. I have never known myself to be so upset. And at last, when he thought he could shut the doors and go off to the presbytery to eat his supper, I approached him near the confessional box.

"You should be ashamed of yourself!" My voice was throaty and low. He looked bewildered. "Who do you think you are, at a time when people are trying hard to return to their faith, abstaining from communion, thinking out their problems, to do what you did in the manner you did?"

"Well, I did wonder if it would be a bit severe," he answered.

"Severe!" I cried. "Do you know, Father, what is going on in the world?"

"There is too much leniency," he said. "The Church must state its position."

"Yes, you are entitled to do that," I answered, "but there are certain ways of doing it—some compassion surely must be shown, some human understanding, like Christ. Did you think of the *people*? Did you try to put yourself in their shoes?"

"I could soften it a bit for tomorrow's Mass," he said.

"Tomorrow is Monday. Who's at Mass on a Monday? You'll just be preaching to the converted tomorrow."

"Okay, I understand what you're saying," he said.

I mumbled, "Good luck," and went out into the cold night, my heart thumping and my head pounding. At least, I thought, I let him know—at least I tried to balance the power. I went on to dinner with a friend who said to me, "Why do you go to Church at all?" I could only answer that I did not know why I had gone to *that* church at all, as I did not want the young priest to destroy my need for the Mass and the Eucharist—as he may have done for some of those around me.

In my optimism I hoped that my stern words might have had some effect. But when I went back two weeks later he spoke again and he had not changed. This time the Gospel was the parable of the Good Samaritan and his Homily was made up of a series of illustrations of how he, as a priest, played the role of Good Samaritan in the city centre by handing over drug addicts and alcoholics found scattered around the cathedral area to the inner-city mission. It was an indirect plea for funds to carry out his good work with the poor. The whole thing was disgustingly self-congratulatory. I swore never to return to a service there again and I haven't.

I wondered afterwards what I had learned, if anything, from the experience. I realized that the fact of speaking out was important, regardless of whether or not it had any immediate effect. Silence of the lay is what is usually expected and accepted, and because of this I feel it is absolutely essential to speak up. John and Lyn did not speak up, and they were swallowed up. If we act as if priests possess superhuman powers, we will be unable to promote the idea of secular and sacred equality. We in the cathedral were without a doubt not being considered in the Homily—we were being abused. We must, as in any democracy, stand up for our rights.

Priests are human, like us, and we are all free-thinking, all capable of sin. I realized later that the Mass in the cathedral was in fact quite riddled with sin: Imp committed a sin in not considering the needs of others and I committed a sin in not forgiving him, because apparently he knew not what he did. Perhaps the greatest sin of all, though, was the collective one.

Those who despised what he said and how he said it still sat—subdued no doubt by reverence for the collar, the word, and the place of worship—instead of walking out or otherwise reacting. This incident gave me perspective on how short a way we had come on the road to equality. One attraction of Catholicism is the surety of moral conviction. But if one is a Catholic drifter, and one is coming to or considering returning to Catholic practice and affiliation, the laying down of rules and the assumption of obedience is not the kind of moral lesson one seeks.

It cannot be refuted that much more open dialogue and understanding between the clergy and the laity are necessary for the future of the Church. But since Vatican II, progress towards this has taken a strange direction, a direction strongly influenced by fundamental Christianity. The growing power of evangelism and its hold over the media have influenced the manipulative practices of a sort of pseudo-liberalism in Catholic parishes. These practices are rudimentally grounded, though, in the politics of the right, and a fundamental streak is invading the presbytery, and infiltrating parish services. The results are visible—arms are raised up in prayer, cheerleaders say Mass and give Billy Graham–like Homilies; a participatory element and a looseness have altered the traditional form of the Mass as we knew it. Hymns are sung to the accompaniment of strumming guitars, and the hymnals are full of gospel-style songs. We are now "Followers of Jesus"—yeah—"thanks to the Lord"—yeah—and we clap our hands a great deal. The atmosphere is optimistic and happy-go-lucky. We see no evil and hear no evil, and we pray together—alleluia—and we-don't-quite-know-why-we-are-doing-it but—alleluia. There is no time to contemplate our consciences or attempt private prayer, or even ponder the Lord's word. We unthinkingly put the words of the Gospel to a simple rhythm. Is this part of contemporary Catholicism attractive to those who are reacting against the old restrictive style of religious practice? A number of Catholics

I know who welcome change say no. They have noticed that today's recruits to the priestforce need not understand classical theology, but are expected to be more attuned to the psychology of cult groups—and that the celebration of the Mass has become more like a circus, with the priest as ringmaster.

Joan commented, "I've noticed recently that the young seminarians at the university church are very mannered—I'm not saying they're gay, but they exude a puritanical asexuality. I can't say there's anything wrong here. But it seems that as soon as a priest of the old school departs to marry, his place is filled by one of these amorphous types." This group of fundamentalists is bred and fed on the motto, "Keep the community happy, the priests in line, the law enforced, and the money flowing in." It is couched in such a fashion that it seems to the ordinary people that the members of this group are liberal, open, and accessible. But in fact there is little personality permitted, no individualism, and creativity is non-existent.

However, as the Church today faces a critical shortage of recruits to the clergy, it is now easy for anyone who signs up to be accepted. If the vow of celibacy were eliminated, the type of person we see as a priest might also change dramatically. But eliminating celibacy is as much wishful thinking as the idea of women priests. The traditional patriarchal makeup of the Holy See is such that abandoning celibacy would seriously shake Rome's old foundation. Allowing priests and nuns to marry would only give more freedom of expression to clergy at the diocesan and parish level, making it harder for the Vatican to control its forces.

The contemporary Roman Church is now made up of groups of extremes—like a pendulum it swings widely between rigid, capitalistic, right-wing groups and socialist, fundamental, and liberal groups. There's a war among them all over questions about the future role of the Church and its clergy, of the laity, of dogma, of traditional practice, of women, of policy and ethics.

And there, far to the right, are the powerful enforcers of Roman Catholic retrenchment—a group made up not only of clergy but of lay as well: the members of Opus Dei.

## Going about God's Business

Every Catholic I interviewed held up the Jesuit organization as one they thought they could respect. It was once the epitome of liberalism and intellectualism, and was known for its strong views which sometimes conflicted with Rome. But it seems now that the Jesuits, as an independent force to be reckoned with, have lost their prominence, due partly to the Vatican's retrenchment. Instead there exists a special intelligence force, made up mostly of priests from a number of denominations from the old way of thinking, who work on behalf of the Vatican as religious headhunters. They concentrate their efforts on promoting the idea of belonging not only to the priestforce, but also to a more secretive club—a sort of central intelligence agency. In short, Opus Dei— "God's work". What better way to make sure that the word of Rome—the status quo—is spread informally yet effectively throughout the world of business, than through an organized network of highly charged and disciplined Catholic intellectuals?

The marriage of money, power, and religion—under the rubric Opus Dei, and in the guise of poverty, chastity, and spirituality—was an idea dreamed up by a Spanish priest in 1928. Members of this society are believers in the corrupting influence of Catholic liberalism, which they obviously do not see as God's work, and they consider the practice of daily Mass and secret meetings, and the role of crusader and martyr, the modus operandi of salvation and sainthood. They are guardians of a sort of civil Catholic religion which recognizes the Church as headquartered in Rome but does not tolerate progress in ecumenicity; they are intelligent, usually capitalistic, and highly moral believers in sacrifice and self-mortification, finding the idea of a club within a club exciting and personally challenging. Their recruiting takes place not only within their own networks, but also through schools. Outstanding students in Catholic schools are not protected from the approaches of Opus Dei. Their clubs and meetings are disguised so well that nothing religious is apparent until the possible recruit is snared in the web, and by that time, with mentors and spiritual leaders in place, the young graduate—feeling the need to belong to something outside the home—withdraws from his or her family and any healthy social life he or she may have had, either to pursue a celibate existence as a priest or nun, or to be a lay member. Stories of parents' attempts to reach their children captivated by Opus Dei are as fearful as similar tales about the Moonies.

I have flirted with the idea of pursuing an association with Opus Dei. That in itself frightens me enormously. The initial attraction of Opus Dei is not hard to see—it is like a drug which one fears can become an addiction. Opus Dei suggests intellectual satisfaction, and a conviction and perhaps a connection with the traditional aspects of monastic life. I have also thought of joining an international organization of Christian businesspeople which gives seminars on ethics in business today, and whose papers and reports intrigue me, because I am pursuing, like most questioning Catholics, a sort of Catholic excellence, and am not necessarily finding it in the old familiar confines of Church, Catholic teaching, or, in most cases, the clergy. But I stop short when I remind myself that being a Catholic requires not only the inner strength to stay with one's own beliefs, but a commitment to them. My need to belong to a club within a club perhaps comes from my inability to find a community through regular attendance at Mass, or even in parish activities, any more, especially now that so much of what I despise—bad music and evangelical ceremonies—has infiltrated Roman Catholicism. I have found camaraderie instead through candid discussion with fellow Catholics who've come to terms with themselves and what Catholicism means to them. These people are neither right nor left; they sit in the middle. They are the Church, the stronghold, the spiritual stabilizers. I will share their experiences with you in the next chapter.

# 10

# PERSONAL REFORMATION

"Religion requires more than simply coping—it
compels us to change."

– DAVID MALL, *In Good Conscience*

I recently had dinner with a close friend to celebrate her fortieth birthday, and we hotly debated whether the phrase "Life begins at forty" had any validity. She wasn't all that hopeful, but what she was sure about was that she had been alive long enough to get to know herself at last—her own limitations, her weaknesses and her strengths—and that did give her a feeling of liberation. She could finally say goodbye to pretence. "You know," she said, "I now have the attitude that, well, if you don't like me, I'm sorry, that's just the way I am."

Driving home afterwards, I went on debating with myself whether reaching forty was a liberation from past angst, or whether it was just the beginning of another stage. The question "Who am I now, today?" is irrelevant unless we add to it "Where am I going?" I know I would feel uncertain if someone directed that question at me. I might prefer it phrased, "What do you intend to do with your life?" because the answer is a whole lot easier: "Improve it."

I once tuned in to an open-line talk show on the radio, where listeners were calling in their answers to the question "What is the point of life?" Most said, quite simply, "To be happy." As a Catholic brainwashed in "old school" attitudes, I assumed that death was the point of life because this life is not meant to make us happy—that state is kept in store for us in the next life, if we're lucky. But if the truth be admitted, regular bouts of happiness are what I seek and wish for in this life. The situation is complicated for us, however, as Catholics. We were brought up and conditioned to live a life of suffering, so it sometimes seems embarrassing to admit that we are happy. For instance, I find I cannot reply to the question "Are you happy now?" I can only recognize that I *was* happy at some period in my past. Happiness to me is not a word to describe a feeling in the present; nor is it a state I can or should feel entitled to in the future. Conditioned as I am not to feel happy, I tend to see the pursuit of happiness as an act of sin and selfishness. So when I am rewarded with a day of contentment or a day of achievement and have a sense of well-being, I feel guilty, fearing that the good feeling isn't something I am entitled to and is really only a calm stretch of water in the middle of a stormy sea. Then again, during these times I find I am more capable of Christian behaviour. Because I am loving myself I have strength and energy to love others. But disillusionment sets in when I remind myself of the parable of the Pharisee and the Publican in the temple—the one in which the Pharisee is up at the front altar praising the Lord and thanking him for his good fortune, patting himself on the back for having abided by the law, while the suffering Publican hovers at the back by the door, afraid to enter, murmuring his sins and asking the Lord for forgiveness. I then become morally confused. How can I be happily confident about my actions and combine this with the Christian prerequisite of humility? It would be out of character for me not to attempt a combination of the two. It is mildly comforting to learn that this dilemma is common among Catholics. The writer C.S. Lewis felt that

> Everyone *feels* benevolent if nothing happens to be an-
> noying him at the moment. Thus a man easily comes to
> console himself for all his other vices by a conviction

that "his heart's in the right place" and "he wouldn't hurt a fly", though in fact he has never made the slightest sacrifice for a fellow creature. We think we are kind when we are only happy: it is not so easy, on the same grounds, to imagine oneself temperate, chaste, or humble.

So what do we do? In his book *On Happiness*, Teilhard de Chardin offers some guidance on the ways we can overcome our feelings of guilt by recognizing the various forms that happiness can take. The first is a happiness based on a state of "tranquillity", achieved only, he says, by a person with a "minimum of thought, feeling and desire", someone who has become immune to harm and hardship by developing a "protective skin". The second is the happiness of "pleasure", which he sees in people who make use of opportunities as they arise in their lives—"savouring the moment" but only waiting for it to introduce itself. And the third is a growth and development attached to a person who finds joy as "an added bonus" to life. "If we are to be happy we must react against the selfishness which causes us either to close in on ourselves, or to force our domination upon others." Instead, he advocates a sort of pioneering procedure—a getting on with life out there in the world, with vigour and renewed spirit, but "in the first place making and finding one's own self."

I looked up the synonyms for "pioneer" in my thesaurus, and while I felt the words "traveller", "pathfinder", "migrant", and "wanderer" were applicable to a person on a journey of selfless self-discovery, I found the assortment of other nouns such as "bum", "vagabond", "vagrant", and "hobo", as well as "pacer", "hiker", "foot-slogger", and "somnambulist", befitting. I pictured a motley crew of Catholics drifting about in their own styles and at their own pace, ending up not where they started but, with luck, nearer to an understanding of their perception of God. They notice the signs along the way, they hear the voice of

God through their consciences, because this road they meander along does not point to the end of their trip, but to the beginning of their life. Identifying God and entering into a partnership and commitment with God perhaps take the form of de Chardin's third state of happiness—that of growth and development. An exciting, painful, and fearful challenge.

One 45-year-old Catholic woman told me, "I think that my fear is present because of my lack of trust. We were taught at school that God is all knowing, all loving, but we didn't know anything about the *person* of God, and our relationship with Him. I find it difficult to have a relationship with Christ the way some of my friends do. My vision of God is a Blake version—God the Father. I'm trying now to develop a personal relationship but it's very hard. I feel I know all the ideas and concepts, but I don't know the person—and that's really what matters."

I asked her whether it would be easier for her if she contemplated God as a human, like Christ, for instance, but she answered that even with Christ she knows that He is also God, so she still feels inferior. "I can't speak to Him, or look Him in the eye, if you know what I mean," she said.

I found that many of the Catholics I spoke to who had drifted away from organized religion voiced the same common problem. Father Lewis commented, "It is a social problem, not necessarily only a religious one. It is not a matter of faith, of the Catholic Church or any other tradition laying anything on them. I find that the dominant problem today is a sense of personal inadequacy, of poor self-image. A tremendous number of people suffer from guilt resulting from insecurity—usually the under-fifty crowd. I find the younger the person, the more insecure he or she is likely to be. Perhaps they have a different experience of the Church than those who have been in it for ten or twenty years. I find that the people who are most self-aware in a religious sense have probably been through the changes within the Church, stuck there through Vatican II to the present day."

Those of us who drift away from organized religion get out of the practice of praying and giving a special time to God in the week. The drifters have not undergone a detoxification of the old childhood scripts that would enable them to develop an open trust and belief in the individual ways of God. It is quite normal to suffer from personal insecurity, fear, and doubt if one is in the process of withdrawing from old diehard habits and beliefs. And if we have departed from Catholic practice, we're bound to feel equally guilty about contemplating a return. Such guilt is also associated with what is perceived to be past abuse of not only the institutional Church, but God too. Yet the chains of old Catholic indoctrination and the habits of a religious past have to be shaken free if we are to experience any form of enlightened liberation.

Brian, who is forty-six, had a Jesuit upbringing; he was educated in an all-male Catholic school between the ages of seven and eighteen, and found that he had to rid himself of his childhood belief in the importance of denial. He had felt, right through his early adulthood, that he had to deny himself—the person he was, his own feelings. So he taught himself "not to have them any more". I asked him what started him on the road to rediscovery ten years ago.

"Well," he said, "it was partly a result of the human potential movement called Shalom, which had its roots in the west coast of the United States. The idea originated with psychologists working on the subject of human existence—and the necessity for people to discover something new about themselves. I started going to these Shalom weekends. They were sort of workshops, conducted under the auspices of the United Church actually. They were humanistic, and concentrated on stuff like empathy and self-actualization. For instance, on the subject of empathy, what was really necessary was to be able to listen to someone else's problems and through doing so find personal enlightenment."

I asked Brian whether for him this Shalom activity had in a way replaced his commitment to traditional religious practice.

"I didn't see the Shalom activity as a religious activity at first, because it wasn't using religion the way I was brought up to use it. But it was in fact using it in a much more real, personal sense. It was Christ-directed. It too asked us to examine our individual sins, if you want to call them that—the 'deaths', the little things we do in which we kill ourselves. I began to understand the concept of sin as cutting myself off from God: He seeks me and I cut myself off from Him—the ultimate divorce. But what I realized too was that in cutting myself off from Him I was also cutting myself off from people in the world around me, and refusing to accept them.

"A lot of these feelings were based on my fear of rejection—that was one of the big things in my past, that I feared my love would be rejected so I feared to love even myself. So in Shalom I didn't associate these feelings with God as much as relating them in a human sense. I began to understand that I was afraid to accept God's love because in my own neurotic, human way, my response to human love had been to cut myself off so I couldn't be hurt again. And if I couldn't love in a human sense then I couldn't love God either, and I couldn't accept His love in return. I think that was my sin—fearing rejection—to cut myself off in whatever way I could, basically killing myself. I realized then that that is what confession is about—healing those dead parts, bringing them back to life.

"Because I had found out what confession meant and what communion meant to me in a very real sense through these United Church activities, my reaction was to blow the Catholic Church because it never seemed to offer the things I needed. But more recently I've come to feel that the Catholic Church has a lot going for it and maybe the answer is to get back in there and try and change it, maybe not very much, but if everybody gets back in there and starts to work on the idea that, 'Yes, maybe we don't have all the answers,' the communication barriers between the clergy and the laity and also between the people together could be dropped. You see, I think God works through His people, and the only way I can know more about myself is through someone else. And Catholics do have a lot in common—similar beliefs and doubts and questions—so we should help one another."

When I first started talking to Brian about his renewed desire to come to terms with Catholicism, I knew about his old interest in Californian pop psychology. In fact, I had had a habit of sneering at it. Everybody is entitled to find his own way to God, and Brian did so in what could be perceived as self-indulgence, but at least he identified the barriers of his past and made a healthy attempt to break them down.

Joan, who is married to Brian, shared the experience of the Shalom workshops. She says, "For me those weekends were really a validation of myself as a person. The good parts of me and the bad parts. They helped me to accept my incompleteness and my negative parts. I had been taught at school that there was a 'good Joan' and a 'bad Joan'—the good one we'll accept and the bad one we'll reject. So the whole of my life, at home and at school, I had rejected that part of me which didn't live up to other people's expectations, I had denied that part of me, and I wouldn't accept it. Those weekends helped me to work on getting myself together as a whole person, not in two parts. It's hard to accept I can be vile and bitchy!"

I realized then that there is another element to be reckoned with in our search for God, and it can cause more pain than anything else. That is, not just fearing Him, or not trusting Him, but waking up to the fact that we're capable of also having a relationship with His arch-enemy—the Devil.

## Deliver Us from Evil

One of the most vivid fears of my childhood was the pervasive presence of the Devil. Slowly, as I grew older, I managed to

175

dispel thoughts of the horned creature or the black shadow. But as an adult pursuing a relationship with God, it would be rather naive of me to deny his existence.

Christ, during his life, had the Devil constantly springing out and bargaining with him at the least expected times. But perhaps it wasn't too surprising. After all, as human beings we're tormented regularly by the conflict between the forces of good and evil within us. Such conflict is only natural and our awareness of it should not paralyse us with guilt. I found novelist Piers Paul Read's comments in *Why I Am Still a Catholic* illuminating on the subject:

> I was conscious from quite early in my life of a capacity for evil which by confirming the diabolical made it easier to accept the divine. Novelists, by the nature of their profession, reveal more about themselves than most men; and the facility with which perverse and depraved characters have come to life in my imagination has demonstrated to me my own potential for evil. I am always conscious of the conflict between good and evil within myself; and in the last analysis I believe in God and in the grace of God because I am not what I might be.

What he says proves to me how easy it is to slip between good and evil—God and the Devil—quite regularly. If I ignore this reality, trusting completely in God's guidance, I may quite possibly head off in the wrong direction, thinking I am going the right way. So how will I be warned when temptation hits? If, as Brian said, God works through others, surely then the way to recognize evil in ourselves is to be able to recognize it in others. But how difficult it is to do so—and how unChristian! Yet evil can only be humanly present when there is a total absence of love: the love of forgiveness, humility, and selflessness shown by a person such as Christ. In the Second World War, this lovelessness caused someone to scribble on a wall in Auschwitz, "Where is God?" Another hand scrawled below, in answer, "Where is Man?" That bleak question will remind us for all time that we all partook of evil, if not as participants, as witnesses to it. All mankind played a part in that devilish plan. The blame for the Holocaust cannot rest solely on Adolf Hitler and some members of his Nazi party, nor even on those who turned a blind eye, or those who feared personal retaliation and did not have the moral strength or trust in God to cry halt. We all stand accused.

But for most of us, it seems hard enough just to be aware that evil exists, or to be prepared when temptation manifests itself. The curse of humanity is not a constant state of lovelessness but a constant state of fatigue, when in short moments of time we forget our neighbour's feelings. Our dilemma lies in attempting to discern between acts of grave evil and ones caused by mistake or error. For instance, is it an act of evil or a sin of omission, or error, to take the vow of matrimony and then break it? Common sense dictates the latter. But many Catholics, when they make an error or mistake that involves not only others but God as well, excommunicate themselves from Catholic association and practice, believing that they have committed acts of such evil proportions that there is no turning back, no forgiveness, no reparation. Some who have excommunicated themselves view their excommunication as the final divorce from all things religious. And their guilt is linked to a sense of having abused not the Catholic institution, but rather God's gifts themselves—the Sacraments. To sin against one or more of the Sacraments is like slapping the face of God.

Father Andrew, the young priest from Boston, recalls a married man who came to talk to him who had been living with another woman.

"The man felt strongly enough about the person he was with now that if he were free they would probably marry. But he was abstaining from the Sacraments. A lot of people automatically excommunicate themselves—we really don't have to worry about the consciousness of sin—there's unfortunately too much of it! There is less of a consciousness of mercy and understanding. With this man I tried to find how he viewed the relationship, spiritually. I asked him, did he feel that this was the right relationship as opposed to the first, which wasn't? People do sometimes discover that they made a mistake, that the present situation, the new love, should have been the first marriage, but because their faith is important to them they ask me, 'How can I be chaste?' 'Should we move out from one another?' I ask them if they think that is right. I say, 'Do you feel as if you are using this other person?' This is a legitimate question in a relationship, I think. 'Do you love?' 'Is there a shadow of a doubt?' 'Are you searching your conscience?' I say I don't care if it is fornication outside the law. The real issue is, is it a real relationship? I can't say—only the people involved can. I try to help them feel absolved, and then to extricate them from the quagmire of believing they are not absolved even when I've said 'I absolve you.' I then try to reinforce and encourage what they feel about their own faith."

Father Andrew told me that many priests are in a dilemma about the high divorce rate and the problems that occur when they attempt to interpret theological teaching, on the one hand, while balancing the emotional needs of the people involved on the other. He spoke of the courage one needs when approaching a priest, even just to talk about one's feelings in such a situation. If a drifting Catholic has weathered the storm of early adulthood alone, and has only bad memories of the old ways of confession, with no knowledge of the new alternatives for reconciliation available in the Church today, he or she will not necessarily feel comfortable entering into a discussion with a priest in a manner which is informal and personal.

"You know," he said, "in our theology there is God within us. But because sitting back, praying, examining our consciences, and thinking about failure is painful, we prefer to busy ourselves with all kinds of things in an attempt to fill the gap—possessions, friendship, work, alcohol, drugs, etc. Keeping busy above all else. But if you examine the whole tradition of the mystic—the dark night, the Garden of Gethsemane, Christ on top of the mountain with the Devil—you realize that you have to go through the crap to get out to the light—to the truth, God, and personal peace. A lot of people feel they don't have the methodology or the means to do this themselves."

I asked him whether he was referring to the process of penance here, meaning a personal reformation, contrition which leads to healing and spiritual renewal.

"Well, yes—of sorts, but penance as an end in itself cannot fill anything. Penance has, in most cases, been done. I find I regularly say to penitents, 'You have suffered, you have done a penance—a personal penance—and maybe now's the time to sit quietly with the scriptures and say some prayers—and if you can't think of any, try the Our Father, which is a prayer filled with all kinds of things. Take the time, let God speak to you. That is not a penance but the way to personal absolution.' "

I was sitting in a church one Saturday afternoon, when confession was nearly over, listening to the quiet sniffs and sobs of a woman a few pews behind. I didn't want to look around for fear of being nosy and everyone around me obviously felt the same way. But then, as the priest left the confessional, I heard her get up and burst into uncontrollable sobbing. The priest took her arm and sat down with her in the pew, and I overheard him telling her she had been forgiven for whatever it was, and absolved. He spoke to me later and said that if a person comes to church clearly asking for forgiveness, it's enough to show that

that person has suffered enough, done penance enough. Even though the woman had not confessed her troubles to him, he added, "It was probably sexual—an abortion, maybe. You know, when I do talk to people I am always extremely moved. I am humbled in my role as confessor by people's sincerity—their honest awareness. Of course, the main thing that comes out all the time is that there is still a great deal of guilt as a result of people just being sexual human beings; that basic human issue is still unresolved and there is so much sexual confusion today— sex is now so highlighted. I doubt there is more sexual activity than there used to be—it's hard to generalize—and it strikes me that people have the same problems as before, but now the problems are much more obvious, partly because of the media, partly because we are more open with one another generally. The problems are there—in the air. Everyone talks about them more."

I asked Father Paterson, an American priest now in his mid-fifties, how he in his capacity as confessor tackles his role in this age of openness and awareness.

"I choose not to probe—I think it is an insult to people's faith and to their intelligence—but I suggest they make the decision by asking themselves which of the two or three areas of sinfulness is the most significant for them—which really disturbs them and why, and I get them to think about it and then we talk about it. I find that I try not to get into a setting which interferes with the process of being attentive to the person, like a confessional box, so the setting itself does not intrude or become an obstacle to discussion. I am constantly impressed by the strength of self-knowledge. The problem is going from the point of self-knowledge to knowing how to live with your own personal limitations, with sinfulness, which is the human condition. That is the really difficult bridge—and sometimes there isn't a bridge."

Invariably penance, a personal apology to God in atonement for a wrongdoing, seems not enough, and perhaps that is why the idea of the sacrament of reconciliation and atonement, with its formal absolution and assigned penance, has significance to many. The Church becomes a spiritual medical centre of sorts where, if one wishes, one can put to the test one's own capacity for humility. Within the old walls of tradition is new help and hope. The sacrament of confession, which at one time, long ago, was disfavoured and disliked, may now become meaningful and necessary as a process of reconciliation.

I asked Father Paterson if he had any advice for a drifting Catholic about how to approach the sacrament of reconciliation, having lost touch with Church-related ceremonies and protocol.

"Well," he said, "most people still, unfortunately, believe they are only forgiven by God through formal absolution. I find this very frustrating at times. For instance, when I visit a hospital I may find I have to talk about abortion to someone, or someone else mentions to me that they don't live a good family life. These conversations can go on for a very long time, but the culmination is usually for me to say, 'You know, God understands that.' One can say that outside the formality of the confession—that God forgives. I feel that it is a message everyone can deliver, priest or no priest—it is the kind of informal absolution which is so necessary, and the one I prefer."

"What about you?" I asked him. "What do you do?"

"I go to confession myself—it varies, maybe once or a few times a year. When I sense I am really becoming full of self-pity, or I am bothered by sexuality and am using it as a crutch not to face real personal issues, then I feel the need for confession."

"Do you go anonymously?" I asked.

"I do both. I prefer to go to somebody I know, who I think has a bit of wisdom, but that isn't always possible because I am fussy. I like someone I can respect, and it needn't necessarily be a priest or a sister—just another person. If I had a choice it would be face to face with someone I know and respect—like my own spiritual director, who is not a member of the clergy."

181

## Mea Culpa

There are so many stories of Catholics from broken marriages who want to come to terms with Catholicism but feel stymied because of their legal status, or should I say illegal status. But their distress is usually ill-founded, their belief that they have cut themselves off from the Church is hearsay, or a misinterpretation of what is considered right or wrong under divine law. The institutional Church has to take a fair amount of the blame for this confusion, as Father Lewis commented.

"As students of theology training for the priesthood, what we were given as the teaching of the Church was never the teaching of the Church. We were taught, for instance, that if people were separated or divorced they were not allowed to receive communion. That is not true, theologically. It has never been true. That was taught to us, to pass on, so people would not even contemplate separation and divorce. Theologically, in Canon Law, the only grounds for excommunication is in remarriage after a divorce, when they would not be permitted to receive the Eucharist during Mass—though they could attend Mass. But I think even this has to be reviewed. We were taught that anyone who was separated was suspect and anyone who was divorced was sinful. It was taught to us by the authority of the Church, but it was wrong teaching."

Father Wright said, "You know, most Catholics believe that just being divorced—not remarried without annulment—is a mortal sin. They either never return to the Church, or stay not as a full-fledged member but as a part-participant abstaining from the Eucharist."

One 35-year-old Catholic man I interviewed did just that. He did not know, because of his divorce, what his status was. His reply to my question "So what do you call yourself now?" went like this. "I would say I'm a Catholic—maybe in the old terms, a lapsed Catholic—no, but I'm a Catholic—maybe not in a state of grace—definitely not a Catholic in good, full standing."

I asked him to expand.

"Well, I'm sort of a fellow traveller. I have a respect for the legal aspects of Catholicism, so, because of my divorce, I don't take communion. But if you don't receive communion you can't really call yourself Catholic—that's the whole point of the damned thing. I like the Mass, but as the Eucharist is the whole point of the Mass too, I don't go to Mass as regularly as I would like."

So after hearing this, I put my nose back into the Bible to decipher for myself what the theological stand was, and I came up with a number of nice contradictions. In Matthew 19:8–9 Christ, in speaking to the Pharisees, said:

> For your hardness of heart Moses allowed you to divorce your wives, but from the beginning it was not so. And I say to you: whoever divorces his wife, except for unchastity, and marries another, commits adultery.

And Mark 10:11 records the same message, adding that the accusation of adultery also applied to women who remarried. But much later Paul introduced a gender bias and switched it around again.

> To the married I give charge, not I but the Lord, that the wife should not separate from her husband (but if she does, let her remain single or else be reconciled to her husband)—and that the husband should not divorce his wife.
>
> I Corinthians 7:10–11

As the institutional Church is inclined to form regular doctrinal law according to Paul's letter and sermons, it seems that the sacred status of divorced people today is based not so much on Christian principles of forgiveness, but on punishment for wrongdoing. Father Jones in England said, "The state of divorce has to be understood as a disciplinary decree, not a doctrinal one. So we are not dealing with a question of doctrinal divorce, we are dealing with a matter of discipline, although I think lots of people haven't seen this."

Divorce without remarriage is not a sin in itself, although—like Paul—Canon Law recommends the separated parties strive to return to conjugal life even if one has committed adultery. But that is assuming that the other party is willing, and in most cases the original commitment has been shattered and the marriage has broken down.

If both parties are prepared to spend the rest of their lives without another relationship, they can easily remain within the Church. But many Catholics find they have to turn their backs on the regular practice of their religion when, after separation and divorce, they meet another person they wish to marry. Unable to partake of the Sacraments, they marry outside the institution, in a secular or other-denominational church. This is becoming so common that the Church itself, aware of the possibility of losing vast numbers of its members—and their offspring—has been pushed into coming up with a solution. Annulment of marriage is not a new invention of the Catholic Church, but its increasing accessibility is. Nuns in individual parishes and dioceses are given the job of carrying out the preliminary enquiries and are kept quite busy, what with the paperwork, interviewing the couple, their friends, and family, and building up files on the applicants. How much simpler it would be for the Western Church to adopt the stance taken by the Eastern Orthodox Church (separated from Rome in AD 1054), which forgives one marital mistake and gives people a second chance!

Why then, one may ask, do Catholics have to endure the prolonged and sometimes painful process of annulment?

Generally speaking, because they recognize no other way out, yielding willingly therefore to the rules and the power and authority of the Catholic Church of Rome.

Tony decided this was the only way to go. Divorced and then remarried for the second time outside the Church, he is waiting for an annulment to be granted for his first marriage so that his second can be sacramentally recognized. "I applied for an annulment of my first marriage on the grounds that I was psychologically incapable of fully understanding the significance of the marriage vow. I have a good case, I feel, and it has been accepted. If I get an annulment then legally it solves everything—i.e. I was never married, therefore my present marriage can be valid. If the annulment doesn't come through I have three choices: I can either disown my present marriage—ideally, go back to my first wife, which is probably impossible as she has remarried as well; or become a celibate; or hold on to my present situation and decide in my conscience, if not under Canon Law, that I can actually receive the Sacraments in good faith.

"If I did receive the Sacraments now, I would, like Stephen in James Joyce's *Portrait of the Artist*, be spitting in the face of an accumulated weight of tradition. If my annulment doesn't come through, I have to think about that seriously. And if I cannot resolve it in my conscience, then I will have to say I can't be a Catholic. It is not possible. And like a traveller, I will have to go on and look for other sources of spiritual nourishment."

"Like what?" I asked.

"I honestly don't know what other forms of spiritual nourishment I would like," he answered. "Once you're a Catholic I don't think you really want to become a Protestant. I don't like Eastern religions. So I would have a problem. I think Christianity is a nice balance between the world and the spirit—between the body and the spirit, if you like—an opposed tension. Other religions seem to emphasize one or the other. You see, the essence of Catholicism is a Church where the principle is one of authority, the principle of universality. Now you can question the authority, and you don't have to follow it that much, but I do feel the whole Church hangs together on certain questions of authority, like the Apostolic succession. What makes Catholics different is that we at least recognize that the Pope is a leader—whether you agree with what he says or not—and we are prepared to accept the makeup of the hierarchy. It sets us apart from other Christian religions."

Tony seemed to have put himself unreservedly into the hands of the Church hierarchy—clearly he did not view his Catholicism and the Catholic Church as two separate entities. If he had, it might have made it easier for him to reconcile himself with what he believed, and be ready if his annulment was denied.

"It seems," I said, "that you are betting your whole spiritual well-being on this outcome. Would it be worth talking to someone in the diocese about your personal concerns too?"

He looked very uneasy. "No, because the annulment has to be judged on strict legal grounds."

Tony, an intelligent Catholic, was not prepared to try to bend any Vatican-made rules to help himself. In some ways, he was not at all like me—he needed to be reverent to the authority of the Church, it was what he wanted, what he believed was right.

I went about my research on annulment in a rather circuitous manner. First, I had heard via a Catholic friend that Christine, a convert to Catholicism through marriage, had been directly involved in the procedure as a witness in others' cases, as well as being separated herself, and I knew I had to talk to her. Then I read through Canon Law on invalidity of marriage and interviewed some clerics who counselled for annulments. I felt uncomfortable because I was aware that I was researching a subject which was non-biblical, non-dogmatic, and as usual the more questions I asked the more contradictions seemed to emerge. The legal interpretations were in Vatican hands. There were many unclear areas, especially when children were involved in the breakup of a marital partnership, or when one party did not wish an annulment.

I met Christine for the first time at a party. When I asked for an interview she seemed nervous, but when I got to know her more she opened up and was very forthcoming in her account. We met in her recreation room on a Sunday in midwinter, a suitable time for her as her two children were spending the day with their father, at his house. She told me, "I testified at two annulments. One was a member of my family, the other a friend. The member of the family was a number of years ago and the other was recent, and it's interesting how the process has changed. The first one was long and drawn out and involved a lot of people and it was actually, in my mind, more clear cut. I asked a lot of questions when I testified in that one and I was given very strange answers. With the recent one I asked a lot of fairly similar questions and got a set of completely different answers. For instance, there was a child involved in both cases and when I asked ten years ago what the status of the child would be I was told that in the eyes of the Church, if the annulment was granted, it would be a bastard. This time I was told that the Church does not presume now to comment on the civil status of a child. A child from a legal marriage cannot be illegitimate and baptism cannot be reversed.

"The first one was a bit traumatic since it involved the family. I had to fill out a very lengthy questionnaire. Then I was interviewed personally on tape by a nun who tracked me down, called me at my place of work, and arranged for us to meet at the nearest parish rectory. She had done detailed research before she got to me. She asked questions about whether I had witnessed things, like, 'Did you ever see So-and-so throw a plate of mashed potatoes at So-and-so?' They were really silly questions. At the end of the session on tape, I asked her off the record, 'Could you tell me what the person's chances are of getting this annulment?' She explained that a marriage can be annulled if it can be proved that one or other of the parties showed immaturity—in other words, not understanding the responsibilities of being married. Nothing was said about being a Christian or Catholic—just basic irresponsibility and immaturity. Both of these people were in fact young in age and emotionally very immature. So that annulment went through. One of them remarried outside the Church and had a child before the annulment became final, and after all that he never returned to the Church to be married after the annulment came through, even though he married another staunch Catholic. They had originally gone to a priest and asked him to marry them while they were waiting for their annulment, and he refused, and when the annulment came through he notified them that he could now do it but they just didn't bother to go. However, he baptized their child after the annulment came through.

"Now the other annulment—the most recent one—that was the one that really opened my eyes. This time I was not tracked down, a nun just asked my friend if he could provide some witnesses. So I went through his situation—on tape again. I told the nun I didn't want to give my name or to be officially on the record, but she told me that my testimony had to be recorded officially. Now, the person I was testifying for did not want an annulment. His wife had taken up with someone else and had had a second child with him, but my friend wanted a reconciliation. He approached the parish priest for help in interceding and was told that the priest couldn't help him. Even his parents asked the priest to see if he could help get these two people back together, and still the answer was no. To top it all off, the wife had applied for annulment long before she got legally separated! You can submit your application as soon as the marriage breaks down, but they won't open the file until the legal legwork has been done. In this particular case, then, the file had been there for two years, since they had been separated for that length of time but not legally. The reason my friend finally allowed a divorce to go through, and didn't contest it was because his wife was pregnant by another man. Shortly after the divorce he was contacted by the Church Tribunal at his wife's request. It was complicated for me, giving testimony in this case, because I was on his side. I tried to console him by saying, 'Why don't you just get the annulment anyway? Because if you ever marry again the chances are very high that you will want your children to be Catholic.' When the Church had all the material gathered they had the two of them present in a court, represented by clergy. The clergy presented the case to the Judicial Tribunal, which was made up of a canon lawyer and a psychologist, who was also a priest, but it's known that the canon lawyer makes the final decision. They can decide, by the way, without even talking to the couple, and I knew that on paper my friend's case wouldn't stand up. The result has not come in as of today. He was promised a decision in six months but it's been a year and nothing has come through. By now his former wife has had another child. The whole thing is very messy.

"But something happened with reference to my own situation which astounded me. When the last interview with the nun was over—and I had mentioned that I was Catholic with two children and separated from my husband—she actually asked, 'Have you ever considered having the marriage annulled?' Then she said, 'Don't get me wrong—I'm certainly not trying to drum up business, we've got more than enough to keep us busy.' (You pay about $300 to cover all the paperwork.) I think she sensed I was somewhat troubled. I don't know if it was a Christian act on her part, but even when I answered 'No' she said that I could get an annulment if I could prove that for one reason or another I didn't, particularly when I made the vows, understand or carry out a Christian Catholic commitment, and if I could pinpoint an incident during the marriage that illustrated that I didn't fulfil such a commitment. She listed the other alternatives, like if your spouse is a drug addict, psychotic, alcoholic, etc., then he didn't fill the Christian Catholic commitment either. I wondered whether you could take it one step further—suppose the person sleeping next to you grunted to himself every morning instead of saying 'Good morning' to you—did that fulfil the obligation of a conjugal commitment?

"So if you can't treat each other humanly over every little incident that arises, then it seems that is noted as grounds. She gave me the argument that if the Church didn't believe the marriage had existed, I should be happy and get out of it. I said to her, 'But I know it did—even if it doesn't look like it, according to your terms, I *know* my marriage existed, and I know my intention at the time of the wedding was to uphold that commitment.' So the nun gave me some literature on the whole business. Now, looking back on it, maybe she offered me the prospect of annulment to make me feel easier about practising my faith, but maybe I don't want to feel easier.

"I still look upon myself as being married, even though I am not living a married life. We have been apart for almost four years. The fact that he doesn't live here any more hardly makes a difference from when he did live here. I feel free, I don't have to blame anyone or answer to anyone. But as far as the marriage itself goes, to me it still exists."

I asked if she felt it existed for her husband.

"I don't know. He seems to be fighting very hard to act as if it doesn't. I fully expect one day to get notification from him of a divorce and an annulment. The only way I can see myself getting divorced is if the right person came into my life and I wanted to get married again, but right now I don't see that happening. Of course I would like to have a relationship with someone. I'm lonely, I'd appreciate an adult male companion, but it's hard for men to accept women in my situation. But if that did happen, if I did decide to divorce, I still wouldn't have an annulment because it is meaningless. The Church, having stupidly fallen for the public outcry about the rise in the breakup of marriages, has prostitutcd itself with easy, irrational annulments. It has made a farce of the sacrament of marriage—and of us."

It seems tragic that Christine has so few options. She could of course divorce and still receive the Sacraments, provided she did not remarry. But if she ever wants to begin a new relationship with the blessing of the Church, she will be trapped by her own maturity and sense of responsibility. Had she been an immature bride, she would be able to claim an annulment in good conscience; but she wasn't, and despite the hints the nun gave her she is not prepared to lie and say she was.

What of her claim that the Church, in bowing to the needs of those who wish to remarry, has turned the traditional recognition of a null marriage into a wholesale escape from what are supposedly solemn lifelong vows? Is there any rational basis for deciding, retroactively, that a marriage of several years and perhaps several children was never "consummated", at least in the broadest sense? I asked Father Mayhew, a priest in New York who had been recommended to me by Father Andrew.

"Well, you first have to understand what an annulment is. It is a statement that there is no marriage in the first place. And this can only be because, in some way or another, the initial consent was defective. It could be defective because consent was given under pressure, or it could be defective because of one partner's inability to make a true marriage—through non-consummation or impotence, say. Now, the Church has seen lately that what is true on the physical level is also true on the psychological level. Suppose one partner is a psychopath, which you probably know involves an inability to feel deeply—well, a psychopath is not able to maintain a sustained relationship. If a marriage can be declared not a marriage because of inability on the physical level, the same is the case on a psychological level. You can call it 'no match'."

191

"But surely," I asked, "most divorces occur because one or the other partner breaks off commitment due to emotional pressures?"

"Yes," Father Mayhew agreed, "but with annulment you also have to examine the conditions at the time of the marriage. If you assess the facts as far as you can, and determine that there never was a real basis for a marriage, then there's a case for annulment. The trouble with the whole court procedure lies in the fact that it ignores all the sociological aspects. The decision is made on technicalities, not on the future of children or the actual relationship. I mean, there are cases where the marriage ought to continue for the good of the children, for the good of the wife or husband, for the good of the unit whether or not there's a sexual marital relationship or not. Unfortunately, the Church depends far too much on the technicalities. I'm not talking about annulments where, for example, one of the divorced partners is now into a second marriage. Technically the second marriage is no true marriage—since one of the partners was divorced in the first place it doesn't follow the rules of the Catholic Church—but it must be considered a true relationship since the love exchanged and the concern for new children born into that relationship exist."

Kelly, a New York secretary in her late twenties, has just received an annulment. "In many way, the whole process was an eye opener for me," she said. "I had a priest counsel me and prepare me for it, and he made me literally sweat out my marriage. You know, I thought it had finished years ago, but I found out that it hadn't. This priest's job was to make sure that there was no possibility of going back. I really earned my annulment, so when it came through I believed the marriage had never been a marriage at all."

Linda, who has two children from her previous marriage and is now married again after annulment, said, "It's peculiar—it doesn't make sense, really. My kids are a product of the first marriage, but I see it now as just a relationship, not a marriage at all. I made a mistake—not with the kids, but with my first husband. My new marriage works. There's no wool over our eyes. No teenage romanticism! It's real, and I'm grateful that I was given the opportunity to try it again, properly."

Balanced upon technicalities, the term "marital consummation" itself is open to interpretation. For instance, in Canon Law it is written:

> A valid marriage between baptised persons is said to be merely ratified, if it is not consummated; ratified and consummated, if the spouses have in a human manner engaged together in a conjugal act in itself apt for the generation of offspring. To this act marriage is by its nature ordered and by it the spouses become one flesh.
>
> Can. 1061, 1

It might then be argued that if the sexual act within marriage is accompanied by the use of contraceptive devices, consummation has not taken place.

Father John Hardon of the Jesuit School of Theology looks at this question in his impressive book *The Catholic Catechism*:

> With the rise of modern contraceptive cultures, however, a new dimension has entered the Church's understanding of what consummation means. Thus one of the instructive features of not a few decisions by Rome is the Church's willingness to say that a marriage was invalid if there were proved intention to have only contraceptive coitus. Some analysts of Rome's attitude argue that these are cases of nonconsummation. Others reason that the contract itself is vitiated. The noteworthy aspect of this is that natural intercourse has a sacred character that Catholic Christianity

looks upon as the seal of matrimony and its sign of irrevocability.

The questions surrounding the interpretation of consumma-tion therefore become vital in the annulment procedure. Canon 1061, 2 dictates, "If the spouses have lived together after the cel-ebration of their marriage, consummation is presumed until the contrary is proven."

But it is also clearly written, in Canon 1141, that "A marriage which is ratified and consummated cannot be dissolved by any human power or by any cause other than death."

In the end, we know the truth ourselves, whether or not we entered into a vow of matrimony with full consent and understanding of our responsibilities and commitments, and also whether any consummation of the marriage existed. Taking a vow before God is not quite the same as entering into a bank loan, or buying a house. Material commitments usually have a time limit attached to them. During that time, one cannot simply renege on the agreement on the grounds that one misunderstood the meaning of full consent. But then, keeping a promise to love someone "Till death do us part" is in many cases beyond human capacity. And if the love does not survive, what is left of the relationship?

In the past, less leisured age, romantic love and solid compatibility were not considered as essential to the longevity of marriage as they seem today. We live now in a world of choices which makes the practice of conjugal love even harder. We do not need to rely on marriage for daily survival. Yet, if a second chance at marriage is possible, then to some it offers the hope of starting again, rectifying a past mistake.

Matrimony is, in fact, an area where the Church is beginning to show more understanding and leniency. Thomas Bokenkotter, in his book *Essential Catholicism*, suggests that with the shift from the old-style model of marriage—with the man as bread-winner and the woman as homemaker and child rearer—to the model of companionship and equal partnership, there is now a demand for the couple "to relate at a deeper level of their personalities". This style of intimacy requires a "greater amount of emotional maturity" and can contribute more to resolving stress-related problems that could lead to separation and divorce. Bokenkotter reports that proposals have been made within the Church to "institute a two-stage approach" to marriage:

> The first would consist merely in the exchange of vows in the presence of a minister by those committed to an indissoluble union. The second stage would be reached only when the couple had navigated the rocks and shoals and had reached a truly deep level of commitment. At this point the Church would consecrate their marriage as now truly sacramental and therefore indissoluble.

If this approach were to be introduced, how would the marriage vow be amended? Instead of death, we'd have to vow to love and honour "until our first attempt has proved fruitless" or "until annulment do us part". It would be more advisable then, perhaps, to choose a civil ceremony over a Catholic wedding. At present the Catholic marriage ceremony exists not just to legalize a bond between two people but to bless their spiritual union with God. Matrimony is a sacrament of the Church. To enter into it requires a responsible maturity and understanding of not only the meaning of marriage, but the seriousness of the sacrament.

The Church takes the view that it is better for a Catholic to marry another Catholic, rather than someone from a different religious background. This is partly because two Catholics will share a common background, a "nationality" on which to base their marriage. But it is also because both will have a similar understanding of the sacrament involved. In a mixed couple, not only does the responsibility for maintaining a Catholic marriage fall on the shoulders of the Catholic partner, but the non-Catholic may not fully grasp the indissoluble nature of the bond, and how deeply it has been ingrained on his or her spouse by Catholic education.

Kelly, who has since remarried a non-Catholic, said, "I do get frustrated and fed up sometimes. I have to keep explaining this religion to him as he keeps asking. He finds so many contradictions in the teachings, too, and goes on and on. I wish he wouldn't, because I don't necessarily feel like defending the faith, and I can't really put into words why it's important to me to be Catholic, and what I feel inside."

Of course, there is also the other side of the story. The non-Catholic partner is expected to understand the complexities of this religion, and to carry some share of maintaining it in the family home. I'm sure it was not always easy for someone like my father, who may not have agreed with the Church's aims and methods, to keep to his original promise.

Still, the Church must out of necessity place most of the load on the Catholic spouse. Canon Law sets out the responsibilities without compromise:

> The Catholic party is to declare that he or she is prepared to remove dangers of defecting from the faith, and is to make a sincere promise to do all in his or her power in order that all the children be baptised and brought up in the catholic Church.
>
> Can. 1125, 1

Sandra, who lapsed from Catholic practice in her twenties and early thirties, now runs an interior design service in San Francisco with her non-Catholic husband of three years. "David offered no objections whatsoever about our getting married in a

Catholic church," she said. "He is a Christian but belonged to no particular church, and we found the pre-marriage counselling interesting and fulfilling. I married late—at the age of thirty-eight—and I believe I'm old enough to know that I'm in it for life. Since I've married there is a part of me that is very content because I know I have done the right thing, and I know that with God's help our personal life together will be blessed and helped. I mean, anyone who can enter marriage and say, 'Well, I can always get divorced,' has to be crazy. How can you listen to the words 'Whom God has joined together let no man put asunder,' and not take them seriously? But you can't go it alone.

"I feel I belong to the Church now. I feel much warmer towards it. I think I really have come to terms with myself as a Christian, not necessarily a Catholic, but a Christian. I am someone who believes in God, somebody who feels that God is part and parcel of my life, and we talk to the clergy a lot. Our parish priest once teased us and said David was becoming more Catholic than me!"

This, I believe, sums up the state of mixed marriage today. Whatever religious convictions the non-Catholic partner may hold—or non-religious convictions, in the case of an atheist—it is he or she who must ultimately concede and move in the direction of the Catholic way. Thus such a marriage requires a huge commitment, for one is not only marrying a Catholic—both legally and spiritually—one is marrying the Church itself.

And to what extent does the Church offer on-going help to the couple? Canon Law makes it clear that the clergy have a duty to give assistance to any couple married in the Church, whether the marriage is mixed or not, "so that by faithfully observing and protecting their conjugal covenant, they may day by day achieve a holier and fuller family life. It is the responsibility of the local Ordinary to ensure that this assistance is duly organised." (Can. 1063–4) Yet few couples welcome such counselling unless the member of the clergy offering it has their confidence at least—and, ideally, their friendship. All too often, this is not the case.

In setting out the duties of the clergy, Canon Law stresses the obligations that they have to lay Catholics. They are "faithfully and untiringly to fulfil the obligations of their pastoral ministry" (Can. 276, 2, 1). They are to explain "the unity, stability and duties of the family; people's social obligations and the ordering of temporal affairs" (Can. 768, 2). They are, in short, instructed to provide guidance and support through all the doubts, stresses, and difficulties we go through in this life.

This is an immense responsibility, and it requires more than moral rectitude and good intentions. It requires courage and intelligence—qualities that are hard to find. And it requires a *mutual* relationship of respect and trust, which will remain rare as long as lay Catholics settle for a passive role within the institutional Church.

The question is, what are *we* doing to open up communication? When did we last invite a priest or nun to dinner? It is our responsibility as Catholics, in the effort to gain equality, to take some very necessary steps towards opening up to the clergy. As we have been conditioned to keep our distance outside the church, it is natural for us to be suspicious, maybe even embarrassed, at the idea of socializing with members of the clergy. But this shyness can be overcome—on both sides—if we will just make that first kind gesture.

It could be towards the head of the parish, or a priest whose Homily you appreciated last Sunday. It could be the Sister whose advice and guidance you called on in the past, or who has shown special attention to your child at school. Whatever the reason, relaxing with members of the clergy can be as entertaining as it is rewarding. If nothing else, it lends itself to a broader understanding of the other—his or her life, troubles, loves, spiritual difficulties and concerns. More than this, it breaks down the unhealthy barriers that can exist between the clergy and their community, and brings Catholics together in their common heritage.

# 11

# BEING CATHOLIC

―――――――――――――――――――――――――――――――――――

"As theology contributes to social decisions, those
social decisions are contributing to theology....
Nobody completes a theology, then acts on it. It is
in activity, as truly as in reflection, that people and
churches discover their theologies."

― ROBERT L. SHINN, *Morality of the Market*

So far we have travelled through the eccentricities of Catholic
childhood, the rebelliousness of the teens, and the early stages
of adulthood, exploring the changes that occur. We have looked
at ways of dispelling old myths and hangups from the past,
and focused on the difficulties that are evident in unifying
personal belief with institutionalized religious practice. A new
understanding of what "faith" and "Church" really mean can
only emerge if we part ways with the old Catholic "Church", and
return to it as equal partners.

We can usually gain a personal awareness through the
similar experiences of others, and so I asked many people
about the outcome of their individual journeys in coming to
terms with Catholicism, and whether they managed to form
an equal partnership with the Church. In my own search for
what it means to be Catholic, I found that most people, in
attempting to come to terms with their heritage, look for ways
in which they can carry the Catholic label confidently. This is
why most questioning Catholics today cannot or perhaps will
not answer the question that is often put to them—"Are you
a practising Catholic?"—but prefer the question "Are you a
Catholic?", to which they can answer "Yes". Hans Küng said,
"Being Catholic, then, means being ecumenical in the fullest

sense," and most Catholics I have spoken with feel that the only satisfactory way they can be Catholic is to adhere to the basic rules of Christianity. In acknowledging this more liberal practice, however, a certain understanding and acceptance of the old ways of Catholic tradition and ritual, the mystery of the Sacraments—even the discipline and authority we once so despised—are essential.

Tony, the journalist from Philadelphia who broke away from Catholicism in his association with group therapy and Freudian and Reichian theory, comments, "I slowly discovered a new interest in the Church in my mid-thirties. The glow around psychotherapy was fading—the group was disbanding—and we realized we would not be changing the world. We still had to address the basic issues. For instance, death—and what is the meaning of your life. There was also the love of historical continuity, and the love of ritual.

"The Mass can make a big impression on one's imagination—every Catholic I know can look back, nostalgically or not, to a night in church when you could smell the incense and hear the great organ playing, and see the church bathed in candlelight—a religious experience if you like. But there is a hell of a lot to reconcile when returning to the Church. For me, there was a lot to resolve. I felt, as a result of my experience with group therapy, that there were emotional dynamics the Church didn't understand too well, and reconciling this with the traditional Baltimore Catholicism—morality—was hard. Like what about divorce? What if people realize that they have a really shitty marriage? There is limited help offered through the Church, but it is very limited. One is still left with some of the old dogmatic ideals. Reconciling those with contemporary life is what we need to do. Mind you, there is a lot about contemporary life that I don't like. Eighty per cent of my experience with therapy—the human potential movement—was pure self-indulgence. Like the other day, when I overheard a discussion about a new translation of

201

the Bible from the National Council of Churches, in which they are removing all the masculine gender, which is causing them a lot of problems. I mean, how can you rewrite scripture? Like it or not, the masculine gender is a part of it. But despite all the problems, my feeling is that the Catholic Church has a certain strength, unlike the Protestant Churches, because of its authority figures—albeit weak figures, but they are there and they say, 'No, you cannot marry a priest; you can't have women priests.' A lot of these 'nos' are questionable, obviously, but I believe it is a strength of the Church that it is still saying no, so that at least people are forced to understand what the hell they are asking for.

"My concern, then, was my need for a serious religion. I wanted to claim a spiritual heritage that went further back even than the Middle Ages—though perhaps it is as much cultural as spiritual. I like the integration of the two: the cultural side is nurtured by the spiritual—the Church is the museum piece.

"I am presently trying to hold to a spiritual discipline— I think it is necessary if you are serious about religion. The appeal of Catholicism is that it has several varieties of spiritual discipline. For example, you can meditate, in a more Eastern tradition, and still feel a member of the same Church as those who say the Stations of the Cross. I like the idea of worshipping with people of different temperaments."

I thought that at this point I would go back into the past and look for some comparisons, to see why others had committed to Catholicism at times when there was just as much political turmoil in the institutional Church as there is today. I had pored over the writings of St. Augustine, but I was looking for something simple and straightforward—perhaps a testament to the way of Catholicism.

Up sprang Edmund Campion—a familiar name to the English—writer, teacher, and eventual martyr to the Protestant movement in Reformation England. He had ten reasons for being Catholic—which he published in secret in 1581.

1) Holy Writ
2) The Sense of Holy Writ
3) The Nature of the Church
4) Councils
5) Fathers
6) The Grounds of Argument Assumed by the Fathers
7) History
8) Paradoxes
9) Sophisms
10) All Manner of Witness

These reasons reflect the faith of just one man in the six-teenth century—yet there is a similarity to the reasons given today. British journalist, broadcaster, and eminent writer Mal-colm Muggeridge, together with his wife Kitty, converted to Catholicism fairly late in life, and one of his reasons for doing so was the sheer survival of the Church through time—the en-durance of a community of Catholic peoples. St. Augustine's *City of God*, which Muggeridge refers to as a "blueprint for the emergence of Christiandom from the ruins of the pagan world", was yet another reason and influence upon him, and, be-yond St. Augustine, his special relationship with Mother Teresa of Calcutta. The fourth reason was the Catholic Church's re-sponse to world crisis. But in the end, he felt above all the pull of nationalism—the "sense of homecoming, of picking up the threads of a lost life, of responding to a bell that has long been ringing, of finding a place at a table that has long been vacant."

Anders, a retired Austrian businessman in his late sixties, converted to Catholicism after spending the war in England. He told me, "I am what I am and where I am after a long voyage. At any given moment you are beginning. For some people there is a simple certainty, but throughout the history of Christianity and Catholicism you have had others who recognized that for any insight you have into any answer, there is a question. That doesn't cancel out the relevance of the insight or truth, but I suppose it is the nature of the truth that it can never be grasped, as it is so vast—so profound, if you like. I am a convert—I came to Catholicism in my late twenties—a long time ago, very much against my will. I was at the time exploring Quakerism— a very loose form of Christianity—but gradually the beauty of the symbols of Catholicism and the deeper meanings that they had—even the dogmatic way of thinking—got the better of me."

I asked him how he feels now, nearly forty years later, about the decision he made.

"I couldn't be without it. It is the centre of my life. But I think it was relevant that I was living in Canada at the time (in the fifties) and Canadian Catholicism was in part terribly rigid, and inevitably in the first stages one took part in all that. I was fortunate though because I was a part-time student in Toronto at the Institute of Medieval Studies, which was the centre for some marvellous thinking. I was very lucky to mix with the people there and to absorb freely what they said. It was the purest form of Catholicism, really, and I did not shed it until about ten or fifteen years later, when I read a lot and talked a lot and began to see a much more dynamic Church. So when Vatican II happened in 1965 it seemed very much a natural thing to me and certainly I was one of the lucky ones to whom it wasn't a shock. It was what one had thought about, in a very minimal way, and perhaps contributed to as one of the countless people who created the climate to which the Church was responding. In the end, though, Catholicism is the denomination that just happens to suit me. It is a religion which congregates the transcendental and the mystical with a great richness of outward signs and a degree of order and coherence."

That summarizes, perhaps, why Catholicism as an organized religion has survived through turmoil and time. The outward signs are evident in the oldest Catholic ritual, the Mass.

Theatrically, it contains a satisfactory order—a beginning, middle, and end—like the form of a symphony. The focus and the reasons for the Mass are to set up a communication between God and the people gathered together—a public affair—as well as to provide a framework for the celebration of the sacrament of the Eucharist—the spiritual nourishment which in itself is a more personal and private affair.

Irish Tess, whose father, now deceased, was the initial reason she remained Catholic, says now, "I tend to go to Mass as a kind of self-discipline. To me it is a way of life. It is a means of getting up on a Sunday morning. It is a focus in my week. Particularly now that I am not at home in Ireland but working for a while in Boston, and find I lack the support of family and friends, it is nice to keep in touch with something I am familiar with. I go when I feel like it, though—I usually go to the big ceremonies. I always go for Easter and Christmas and occasions like that. I tend to go for Lent. I approve of Lent. I approve of having a time of year when you reassess your life and think of what you are doing."

But while the Mass can be a positive discipline, it can also—for some of us—become boring with constant attendance. I accept those periods of boredom as natural, especially since they are usually scattered between periods of enlightenment. But one Easter I found myself wondering if this boredom was natural at all.

I had been asked to play the organ in a small Anglican community. I had jumped at the opportunity only because I knew that the organ they had in their church was much grander and more sophisticated than the one I was playing in a poorer Catholic parish on the other side of town. I was not particularly inquisitive about the Anglican service itself, thinking it alien to the Roman Catholic Easter Vigil service I was expected to attend later that evening, a moving ceremony where the Church celebrates the new liturgical year, symbolizing renewal through a candlelit service. But the Anglican service began the same way—by candlelight—and since the congregation was smaller, probably because the people who were there really wanted to be there and were not forced there from fear of sin, there was an informality which appealed to me.

We were asked to gather in a semicircle around the altar, were introduced to the ministers by first name, and even the Gospel readings, which were considerably shorter than the lengthy ones I was to contend with later, made the same impression and had the same effect—perhaps more so in their abridgement. I found the ceremony simple and sensual. We each contributed our own particular prayers—in the offertory equivalent of the Mass—but when it came to communion I felt a foreigner, an outsider, as I had been conditioned to in the past. I had been led to believe that for me, as a Catholic, to partake of the Anglican Eucharist would be bordering on blasphemy. I had been taught that Anglicans acknowledge the bread and wine as symbols of the body and blood of Christ, where Catholics accept a literal transformation. In this church, however, instead of the mass-produced grey-coloured hosts of the body of a Catholic Christ, a large French baguette was brought out and broken among us. Suddenly I found myself munching away with the people in the semicircle, and the significance of the Last Supper finally hit home. I was at last experiencing what the Mass is all about—the way it is meant to be. At the end of the service we were invited to stay on at the back of the church, where food and wine were served, instead of being summoned to an overlit basement hall, which is what happens in my parish. In this parish the church itself was the meeting place for the community, and I felt no irreverence in sipping alcohol, laughing out loud, and chatting away on secular subjects. Only when I left the group, grudgingly, to offer my services to the Catholics, did I feel that I had had a religious experience—the sort of feeling I would like to have every Sunday. I scolded myself for being overly romantic, but after the two hours of tedium that followed in the Catholic church, through a service that resembled a clinical operation, I decided I was wrong in thinking that I had been romantic at all. I began to wonder whether I should leave the Catholic fold and join the Anglican parish. Their work within the inner city, the social services they offered and their concerns and outward energy, reflected what I felt a parish should be, and the ministers did not look down their noses or try to take superior positions within the service, even in the extracurricular activities.

It was only after much deliberation that I realized that my God would be the same in either church, and that it was unnecessary for me to change denominations. Instead, for the first time, I recognized the richness of combined Christianity. I remembered that "unity" and "ecumenicism" had been words used regularly in discussions among members of my mother's *ad hoc* Catholic reform group at the time of Vatican II. As liberal Catholics, they seemed encouraged by Rome's recognition of other Christian denominations as part of Christ's universal church. I'd read reports about the progress being made in this direction but never realized how a unified church could exist in practice. Pope Paul VI's Vatican II Decree on Ecumenicism invited discussion of the doctrinal principles for reunification of Christianity, of the need to recognize that baptized Christians are all part of the spiritual Church of Christ. It promoted a more liberal approach for all Christians to share in prayer, dialogue, and study, and interdenominational services were offered, and many attended.

Through celebrating Easter in an Anglican church and later a Catholic one, I had perhaps practised what had been preached—I had broadened my participation as a practising Christian. I had individually made a step towards unification and had been welcomed by the Anglicans. But would it have been so easy for an Anglican to do likewise—to attend and

207

fully participate in the Catholic service, partaking freely of the Eucharist?

A Catholic lobbyist for unity in London told me, "The problem really is the idea of the true Church. The Catholic Church believes that as a Church of Christ, it is the one and only—Peter's appointment and the Apostolic succession, the power of the cardinals and bishops and their unification to Rome, and the recognition of the Pope as the Vicar of Christ. The reason that many other Christian churches sprang up was that many people opposed this authority and broke away. Now the idea of a new church, as a dynamic community, something not tied to this structure, a sort of universal Christian Church, is not easy to define. People who are doing serious theological work on this subject have not yet come to grips with the idea of a Church without boundary, without passports. They are more concerned with the sorting out of obstacles and form—where do we agree? How do we recognize our faith and each other's faith? Where are the differences? and so on—but not with where this should lead."

The Pope, interestingly enough, often makes a strong impression on people of other religions, who are at arm's length from the problems of Catholic identity, because of his tireless efforts to bring peace and succour to troubled, poverty-stricken areas of the world. Television permits him to be seen not only as a leader but as a man. But if Catholics were to form a united church with other Christian denominations, he would have to be embraced as the spiritual leader. Seeing that the Protestant movement was formed in the first place to break with Rome, it hardly seems likely that Protestant Christians would contemplate rejoining.

Yet, for Catholics, the ecumenical drive has offered many advantages, one of them being Rome's recognition of a more broadly based united Christian people, which makes for more informal and open discourse, and closer relations with other churches.

There exists now a Church of Rome, just as there is a Church of England and Scotland, but this Church is not solely a Roman Church. With the loss of Latin came the introduction of every language. Perhaps the Church of the Catholic people has already arrived at the point of Christian unity intended by Vatican II, for many Catholics who have come to terms with Catholicism have done so by pursuing less restrictive forms of practice.

Joan and Brian have created, through their past experience with Shalom and with the help of other couples they know, a house church. Members include a Catholic and a German Lutheran, two United Church people, a Ukrainian Orthodox, and a Presbyterian.

Joan explains, "The whole purpose of the group is to get closer to each other, and therefore to God, but our differences make up the church. But it is in fact a church, in that we gather together in God's name to give praise."

I asked her to expand on the activities of the house church.

"We are very open-ended. We usually decide what we are going to do before each meeting. Last time we looked at a whole lot of evangelistic books and decided on a course of discussion chapter by chapter."

Brian found satisfaction in the house church since he had had a problem associating his relationship with God on a personal level with the conformist religious requirements of the Catholic Church. He still attended Mass, however, and found that his association with both helped him achieve a fuller spiritual life.

The house church idea seems to be gaining in popularity among keen Catholics. In Holland small informal Catholic communities are springing up within the larger, more formal parishes, where discussions and the sharing of problems and ideas take place, and where sometimes Mass is celebrated. Informal Mass and eucharistic participation are a popular alternative for a number of women in the Church these days, especially nuns and lay involved in social work and teaching. For instance, in America there has recently emerged a Womanchurch, which is a Catholic movement built on support networks between women clergy and female laity, so that some ministry can take place among women, beyond the existing strict structure which excludes women from priesthood. Mary Jo Weaver, author of the book *New Catholic Women*, states that "The key to understanding Womanchurch...is its claim to *be* church." She describes the need women have, not necessarily to exile themselves from the Catholic institutional Church, but to be in "exodus from patriarchy". "We need to think of solidarity as the strategy for survival, not simply as an emotional bond holding women together," she writes. For Catholic women who cannot tolerate the male chauvinism of the institutional hierarchy, for those who feel called to the priesthood but cannot practise, and also for those who just need to question further and can only find an answer within a group of similar-thinking people, offshoot ecumenical groups are the only alternative.

My mother, in England, is a member of a community, made up solely of Catholics, called The Group—an extension of the old *ad hoc*. She still attends Mass every Sunday but finds stimulation and company in this group of thinking men and women. One member commented, "We have people here who are eminent scientists, brilliant in mind. One such person said to me that because he found it most important to look at his own religion through the eyes of someone else, he found it very helpful to share the experiences of other people, to hear what others feel and share their problems."

I asked him whether Rome frowns on this sort of activity.

"It depends on the parish," he answered. "Our bishop is very keen on this. It depends on the archdiocese. I believe that our little community is something different. It has a dimension unto itself. To get together to talk with one other person is something. To share the Eucharist is very much more. To me, that is the main reason why Catholicism is particularly relevant, because of that ultimate sharing and love."

If this trend of house churches or offshoot activities continues, it will be interesting to see how parish priests and heads of dioceses and archdioceses respond. If some bishops view it as a threat to the existing parish structure, then no progress will be made within the Catholic community itself, nor will liberal, questioning Catholics find a forum to air their concerns as well as to celebrate their faith. But if members of the institutional Catholic Church communicate more closely with its parishioners in the search for spiritual comfort, then Catholic people will in turn surely help the clergy do a worthwhile job in promoting Christian work. If this happens we may find a sort of equality of spirit and unity of community emerging, which would provide a strong platform for the promotion of Christianity and Catholicism alike.

Father Jones supports the ecumenical view wholeheartedly. "I see now an image of a pilgrim Church again, similar in some ways to the people who were with Moses in the desert, who wandered around the Sinai Peninsula. I can imagine that at times some felt following the hills would be a better choice, and others argued it would be better to follow the line of the river, in order to have water for the herds. Sooner or later disagreements would get worked out, proving that the clash of ideas is a necessary part of communal life. We've gone in the wrong direction many times. We've gone in circles quite frequently. But we arrive. Catholics either have a rigid idea of the Church, in which they feel they are tied to fixed attitudes, or understand that Church to be a pilgrim Church, where all of us are feeling our way and finding our way together.

"I don't belong to the rigid organization. I belong to the people of God, the people who are trying to find their way.

Obviously the bishops and the Pope cannot be ignored, but they can't be given a sort of superhuman role."

Many converts to Catholicism cite Rome's present structure, its tight, authoritative, dogmatic link, as its main attraction. Yet it seems that if we are to remain Catholic and grow as Christians in the future we must maintain a healthy balance between the original rock of Rome, with its ritual and discipline, and the transcendental aspects of faith that accompany a freer way of Christian life. If the answer is for the two forms of religion to move closer, then—as Hans Küng wrote in *What Must Remain in the Church*—

> The Church will have to be further changed in order to remain itself. And *it will remain what it ought to be, if it remains with him who is its source and foundation*: if in all progress and change it remains faithful to this Jesus Christ. For then it will be a Church which is closer to God and at the same time closer to men.

The cardinals, instead of claiming that the liberal promotion of women to ordination in the Anglican community is a road to fragmentation and a barrier to Christian unity, might instead consider what Christ would have done if put in charge of a parish. Father Andrew had a good idea: "If I were ever a parish priest the first thing I would do is make up little cards saying, I am new at St. Stephen's, or whatever, and my name is Father So-and-so. I would put the names of the pastoral staff too, with a phone number, and walk around the neighbourhood and drop them in all the letterboxes, knock on doors, ring doorbells, say, we are here, we invite you to come, if you have a problem call us any time you want to—come, we are happy to have you. I would try to extend hospitality and the message that we are there to serve the people, to make some home visits, chat for no particular purpose—state clearly that we are not after money, say, we're here to see you, what are your needs and what can we do as a parish? I know I'd get a response from people who need some spiritual communication. We have to say, we're here. If there were some leadership on this from the bishops, if they said, get off your ass, get out of the TV room in the rectory and go pound the beat of your parish—if a bishop gave the challenge, more would rise to it."

How much of the problem, in fact, stems from the Church's inability to communicate to Catholics—to make clear what is important to them and what is not so important in its spiritual and secular values? It seems that as a business organization the Church lacks a unified and on-going effective public relations campaign. In the book *In Search of Excellence*, Thomas J. Peters and Robert H. Waterman Jr. suggest ways by which large companies can work towards a future of growth and productivity, by concentrating on the five elements of "the external, on service, on quality, on people, on informality". If the past excellence of the culture of Catholicism is to be maintained alongside the informality of a broader Christian community, the male hierarchy of the Church will need to relax about the growing force of Catholic women, and they will find their parishes to be better places for it—more efficient, more caring, more nurturing, and more open. Women in the business world do not do a man's job in a man's way. They achieve success in their own style. And the contribution that women can make within the Church is certainly no less than the contribution they are making in the secular world.

I would offer, in summary, that the Catholic Church on the local, secular level should, in part, be independent of Rome, in order for its members to understand and provide for the needs of the people who make up the secular community. We live in an ecumenical world today—a world of mixed races and religions. Christian unity could now finally be put into practice in a way lat reflects the multi-faceted society we see around us on the streets.

Anna—the marathon runner from New York—has found unification by joining a socially oriented Anglican parish. "We have soup kitchens, in which I like to help. There are programs for the elderly, home help, and visiting the sick. The helpers there include some Catholics, Muslim Palestinians, Jews, and a number of atheists, as well as the daughter of the Bishop of Boston."

I can only end on a note of optimism for the future. The generation about which I have written throughout this book—those who've weathered the storms of change from the era of Vatican II to the present—may find religious revelation through teaching their children their own moral and ethical codes of life with no reference to the old Catechism. The Catholicism of our youth, recorded by so many of those I talked to for this book, will seem, as we grow older, more and more like a bad dream, because the era of Catholic convent education as we knew it is over. Our children will probably never really comprehend the Catholicism of their parents' youth. With luck theirs will be more like a "Catholicity" of the kind Küng refers to—a liberal label, a freer style than that of the past "dogmatic construction", which is more in keeping with the message of Jesus Christ, yet "intelligible to people of the present time".

# 12

# THE NEXT LIFE

"Education, besides arousing and developing the
consciousness of our duty to act in a Christian way
in the social and economic field, must also teach
the methods by which this duty may be
performed."

— POPE JOHN XXIII, *Cantagalli*, 1961

A litmus test of whether we have come to terms, personally, with Catholicism is how well we are able to offer religious guidance to our offspring.

Every Christian child has a right to be baptized—to be welcomed into the "club" through the sacramental ritual of cleansing among family and friends—but it is not uncommon for Catholics today to avoid arranging baptism for their young. Some friends told me that they could not accept that their infant was born with inherited sin. But in most cases the real issue is that the parents haven't made up their minds about their own faith, and so are uncertain about launching the child on a Catholic course of education. This concern is not unreasonable given that Canon Law clearly states that, for an infant to be baptized lawfully, it is required

that there be a well-founded hope that the child will be brought up in the catholic religion. If such hope is truly lacking, the baptism is, in accordance with the provisions of particular law, to be deferred and the parents advised of the reason for this.

Can. 868, 1–2

A large number of Catholic parents I interviewed said they had decided to bring their children up themselves, educating them in a basic moral code at home—nothing particular but nevertheless Christian-based, so that the children could "find out" when they grew older what they believed, and make their own choices. But this course can be unfair and unrealistic. If no elementary traditional, ritualistic religion is introduced at an early age, how can children make a choice when they have no terms of reference against which to judge? It is also important for those parents who themselves suffered through their Catholic education to realize that times have changed—and that "protecting" their children from Catholic religious education may be unnecessary when so much has altered since their own bizarre pre–Vatican II school experiences.

I asked Joan and Brian, the house-church couple, about their fifteen-year-old daughter, who had a traditional Catholic school education even though her parents hold liberal views. Brian said, "We educated her in the Catholic faith because we were told that that was what we had to do. Basically part of the law—the rules and regulations. Part of our upbringing. In a way I regret it, as I think Christ's teachings are being misinterpreted by the people who are teaching, but nevertheless—having gone through that process myself, and despite having taken years and years to unravel it and to get down to what it really is about—I think it is still worth it. If you don't have it at all in the first place then you don't have anything to unravel and that is a loss."

I asked them both what they felt about the possibility of it all going to waste, though—whether it might convince their daughter to turn her back on the whole thing, to turn against Catholicism completely. Joan answered, "She can go to another school, if she wants to go to another one now. She has the background of Catholicism. The education has done some good in that it has introduced moral standards. She knows what it's about; now she has her chance to rebel, leave it, rethink it, or explore other things. She will probably want to put it in cold storage for a bit. We're prepared to bet she'll come back to it at some stage."

A Catholic education does, at least, allow for moral standards and traditional symbols to be introduced to the young, enquiring mind. I once read a woman's remark in a parish bulletin that "I want to have my child baptized because in life we need to hang on to something. The person who believes in nothing is completely deprived when adversity comes." I myself believe this to be true.

The question today is, how do we introduce the ways of Christ to a child in a healthy and interesting manner? Ideals of community and Church are still very much a part of the Christian life, but with ever-increasing split-ups of families through divorce and separation, and the growing incidence of mixed marriage between couples with different religious backgrounds, the home setting does not always provide a clear, consistent moral environment.

A friend of mine in New York who was educated as a Catholic, and rebelled, later marrying a Jew, is not bringing her twelve-year-old daughter up devoid of traditional religion, even though she did not have her baptized. Her way, however, seems to be a satisfactory compromise.

"When I had Samantha," she said, "after marrying in a Unitarian church, my mother was very confused. She kept asking me how I was going to raise my child. But by now it's perfectly natural for Samantha to go to a Passover Seder on one day and Mass on another.

"The school she attends is an Anglican one. It just happened to be near our apartment and had the right hours for me as a working mother. It was a harder decision for my husband, as he was nervous that she might become totally Episcopalian. But, you know, she's fine. She has a wonderful voice and sings in the choir there. She has Evensong two days a week, she sings in the service on Sunday, and in the summer she goes to a Jewish camp and takes part in the Jewish services on Friday nights. A lot of her friends are becoming teenagers now—going through bat mitzvah. I don't know what she will decide to do. But as religion is part of her life, I know that her fate will be associated with religion."

The renowned Austrian-American child psychologist Bruno Bettelheim insists, in his book *The Uses of Enchantment: The Meaning and Importance of Fairy Tales*, that it is vital for the modern child to be introduced to

> images of heroes who have to go out into the world all by themselves and who, although originally igno-rant of the ultimate things, find secure places in the world by following their right way with deep inner confidence.

Wondering how small children today are being taught to discover their heroes, I set off with a notebook and tape recorder one winter morning to an elementary Catechism class at a Sunday school attached to a large urban parish church in Toronto, just to see what exactly is going on. As I go inside, carrying the memory of parts of my old 1956 childhood missal, with its threats of eternal damnation and warnings of the awaiting abyss of sin, the first sound I hear is guitars and the haphazard hand-clapping of young children singing songs to Jesus—gospel style, of course. But under these circumstances, the style is appropriate. At least it is better than standing in a line singing, "Lord, for tomorrow and its needs, I do not pray; Keep me, my God, from stain of sin, Just for today," and not understanding what the hell it all means.

I wander in. The children, aged two to nine, are standing in a semicircle, with their parents behind them, around two women who are lay ministers and a priest who is actually strumming the guitar himself. They are being encouraged to laugh and enjoy themselves and answer random questions like "Are you happy?" The kids shout, "Yes!" "What makes us happy?" asks one minister. "Skating and snow," a child replies, and a shrewder one says, "Going to church." After this and more singing, they head into a large classroom with a blackboard and colourful drawings on the wall, and take out their books. This is the Sunday for the Gospel of the Good Samaritan. The children are on the floor around one of the young teachers and are introduced to the idea of "brothers and sisters" by being told that everyone in the world is your brother or sister. "What do we do to help our brothers?" asks the teacher. There is a pause, and much shuffling and wheezing, and one little girl says, "We help with sweeping the leaves." Other suggestions are offered and then the teacher asks, "What do we do when people don't have enough to eat? Do we give our food to others?" One boy shakes his head seriously and says, "No, but you give money to help them." There is a short burst of discussion about how you do this, and where the poor boxes are, and what UNICEF is, and how it helps other children in the world.

A large piece of paper is pinned up on the display board, with the heading "We Are Disciples". The children are requested to contribute their own suggestions about being a disciple and soon the paper carries a long list.

Do good things
I am going to pray
Say good things
I will be good
People are kind
Love God
Enjoy being.

What impresses me about this general introduction to a Christian way of thinking is that I am witnessing the initial attempts, within the learning environment of a classroom, to introduce rudiments of Catholicity.

I join an older group, the nine-year-olds, where they sit at a table with books illustrating scenes from the Old Testament. They are in fact studying the Commandments, the first being

I am the Lord your God, who brought you out of the land of Egypt, out of the house of bondage.
You shall have no other gods before me.

Exodus 20:2–3

They have to write the Commandment down in their scrapbooks and then illustrate it. The illustrations are of Moses on Mount Sinai receiving his instructions from God, and while they colour and draw the teacher asks them to define a covenant. One answers, "An exchange of promises—an agreement." This, I thought, was a pretty good introduction to ethics—what is a promise, what's a vow? Promising to take care of each other, and to take care of yourself.

Discussion ensues about other gods—what other gods? Hands fly up. One little boy suggests "rain gods", another says, "It's not good to worship money."

I spoke to one of the teachers afterwards, who told me that the Catechism is still the essence of early teaching but that it is vastly different from our old "highway code". There is a much greater emphasis put on the stories of the Old Testament—where heroes and heroines abound—on understanding religion and the emergence of Christianity through time. She said that programs for Catholic elementary education have been introduced that are based on research by many modern secular educators on childhood learning, and on how children perceive reality and come slowly to an adult perception. "It is an effective approach, drawing especially on the experiences of each other, of family, on events in their daily lives, to give them some analogous perception of what God is, and of what Jesus is in our lives, introducing them gradually to the use of the Sacraments and the expressions of celebration."

There seems a much greater understanding today of how to teach religious knowledge with a more positive approach to the inner motivations of a child. There is far less negativism than there used to be, much more "thou shall" than "thou shalt not". And the fear of sin, and our capability for evil, ever present in many Catholics' pasts, is refreshingly absent.

I interviewed five-year-old Stephanie on the subject of religion (she attends an elementary Catholic school) and this is how our talk went.

*"Who do you think God is?"*

"He's my father."

*"Could He be a lady?'*

"No, He's a boy."

*"Do you see Him sometimes?"*

"Yes."

*"How do you imagine Him?"*

"You just think hard in your head. And when you don't want to see him any more, you just open your eyes."

*"What does He look like? Does He look like anyone you know?"*

"No. You just let your head see God, and you say prayers to Him."

*"What sort of prayers do you say to Him?"*

"You say nice things about your mother and father."

*"All right, let's pretend I'm God. What would you say?"*

"God, I thank You for everything You done for me. I hope that my Mummy and my Daddy don't fight."

*"Do you think God helps then?"*

"Yeah, and you say nice prayers."

*"Like what?"*

"Dear God, make the flowers come true. Make all the badness be niceness. That's all."

*"When do you say these prayers?"*

"At bedtime. I kneel down by the bed."

*"What about your friends—do you think they do the same as you?"*

"Yes, they do. I try to say nice things to them and then they will say nice things to me."

*"What are the bad things, though? Do you think there are only good things?"*

"Sometimes there are fights at school."

*"Do you fight?"*

"No. Sometimes we fight, though, like playing."

*"So do you think it's a sin to hurt someone?"*

"What's a sin?"

*"When you do something against God to hurt him."* She looks blankly at me—she obviously doesn't understand—so I change the subject. *"Do you know who Jesus is?"*

"God's friend."

*"Do you like Jesus?"*

"Yes."

*"Do you ever pray to Jesus at school?"*

"Yes, we pray to two of them, God and Jesus."

*"Whom do you prefer to pray to—Jesus or God?"*

"God."

*"Do you see Jesus in your mind better than you see God?"*

"No, I see God better."

Stephanie's spiritual understanding at such an early age was quite awe-inspiring! But given my own early training, I wondered if she was being taught in a way that hears no evil and sees no evil, or at what age she would be introduced to the concept of the Devil's existence—if at all.

Father Donovan, Superintendent of Curriculum of the Religious Education program at my local Separate School Board, brought me up to date.

"Personally, I believe the new approach to religious instruction is a healthy one. I myself was educated in Ireland and brought up with the old texts of the Catechism—I remember that method to be very prescriptive and it required an intellectual knowledge of Church doctrine. It was strong on apologetics and rational intellect. But today I think you will find that young people have an attitude towards God that is more relaxed in a good sense—there isn't the same element of fear, there isn't that element of God as judge, and there isn't that element of punishment as the ultimate sanction. However, your concern that the children are being protected against the knowledge of evil—of sin, of Satan and so on—may come from having been educated yourself with a false apprehension about what their relationship with God should be, and is ill-founded, I believe.

"We all learn about sin and evil in a non-theological sense in our own lives. We don't force that sort of thing onto small children. We try to keep things sunny and bright for them. We correct them if they do something naughty or something bad, but we pass over it quickly and accentuate the positive in their lives."

Bruno Bettelheim has shown how a moral education takes place through the telling of stories, particularly fairytales with their strong moral sense, which children can easily grasp and identify with. The message that "crime doesn't pay" is always present in tales where the bad person ultimately loses out to the good, although Bettelheim points out that "a child's choices are based, not so much on right versus wrong, as on who arouses his sympathy and who his antipathy."

Father Donovan agreed with this view. "Gradually, over their years of growth and maturation, children become aware of instincts and tendencies in themselves, and in their companions and in the world in general. They gain an ever-widening knowledge of the notion of evil in the world, which we call sin. And we make allowance, in their religious education, for a similar developmental approach, so they can recognize these matters. But we still introduce the sacrament of reconciliation around the age of seven or eight, so they are in fact already dealing with the concept of sin then, personal sin and the notion of the need to be reconciled."

I was particularly intrigued by the process of preparation offered for confession and communion, and wanted to know what, if anything, had changed.

"Well, I think the rule of thumb the Church has used for a long time is still in force," Father Donovan said, "namely that a child is ready for the reception of First Communion when he or she is ready to distinguish between ordinary bread and the bread of life. They certainly don't have to know about the whole marvellous, unspeakable mystery of God becoming man and being present in the guise of bread and wine. And they certainly don't have to know about transubstantiation. Those terms are not widely used any more anyway. There are other words used now in explaining and expressing the mystery of the Eucharist. So I would say there's enough flexibility there for the children to be introduced to those two sacraments when they are ready, a judgement to be made in concert with the parents, the priest of the parish, and the teacher. That is the ideal trinity of influences."

"But not always the case," I added, "especially when families are often fragmented—either literally or from a religious point of view. I know a number of children who are attending Catechism classes on the weekends and a non-Catholic school during the week."

Father Donovan nodded. "Yes, we do know that very often one or maybe two of those three elements will be missing. And one of the problems we have in our schools is that, for one reason or another, the parents are often not involved. And I have to say the clergy are sometimes not involved with the school or the developing faith of the children either.

"We are really not set up to deal with fragmentation. Our programs are based largely on the assumption that children will continue in a Catholic education right through. Children coming in halfway through will pick up as themes and subjects are dealt with a second time in a more profound way—but that can be difficult for them. We are developing new themes now—and piloting many different approaches."

If children are not subject to the whole culture of Roman Catholicism from their early life, does it mean that their understanding of their religion is incomplete or uncertain? I do not believe so, nor did Father Donovan—it can simply make it harder for them, just as changing schools in mid-stream can cause difficulties. However, early Catholic education has become so much more open and flexible that the next generation of Catholics will probably not need a book such as this, one which attempts to explore the confusion in which a whole generation of Catholics—and more—finds itself. With any luck they will have started on their course of learning with the right attitude, and by the time they reach adulthood will have come to terms, instead of continuing to rebel.

In this regard, I found a nine-year-old boy's concept of prayer enlightening, especially as Simon attends Catholic classes only on Sundays. They obviously hold a novelty for him. I asked him what it was like being Catholic and he replied "It's fun, because you get to go to church and sing songs."

*"When you are not at church, do you think of God in the week?"*

"Yes, when I say my prayers."

*"Do you think of God at any other time—when you are walking down the street?"*

"Sometimes."

*"What does God look like? What do you see?"*

"Jesus."

*"What about any one else—Mary?"*

"No."

*"Who else then?"*

"Moses."

*"Why Moses? Do you like him especially?"*

"I like his stories."

*"When you pray, do you use set prayers, or your own?"*

"Sometimes when I pray I use my own prayers, I just make them up."

*"Do you have a conversation with God then?"*

"Yes."

*"What do you talk about?"*

"My Granny and Grandpa. My friends."

*"What do you say?"*

"I say I miss my Granny and Grandpa, and I really wish they would be here."

*"So what about school? Do you think you are different as a Catholic at school?"*

"No, the same."

*"Does anyone talk about God at school?"*

"No."

*"What about when you grow older, do you think you will become more interested in God?"*

"Yes."

*"Why's that?"*

"Because I would know how to pray better."

## The Continual Study

We are now used to living with technological progress. Yet there is a danger that this progress is displacing the pursuit of higher knowledge, the continued thinking and questioning that should enrich the inner life, the mind and the conscience.

Television is perhaps the greatest problem here; it tends to replace reading, it interrupts conversation, and it generally intrudes on the realms of human imagination. It also promotes a very limited vision of the world, a world where consumerism and materialism are the idols. Nowadays the younger generation expect to receive what they want when they want it—not to suffer, hope, and pray for it, as in the past.

Earlier in this book Father Andrew, journalist John, and Frances, Elizabeth, and Tess spoke of the influence of a parent on their own spiritual education. Today, with the increasing breakdown of the home, there seems to be an urgent need for unified religious conviction within families. Hans Küng recommends we should "continually study and examine the Christian faith afresh"; how can we satisfactorily do this in and out of the home and set an example for our young?

If a parent doesn't go to Mass, can we expect the children to make an effort, or even to understand the significance of regular churchgoing? If religion is not talked about or practised at home, how will spiritual sensitivity be instilled?

The foundation for understanding Catholicism has to be an appreciation of the Church's history and philosophy, and clearly the Church has a duty to promote this. But, as priest and popular writer Andrew M. Greeley wrote in *The Catholic Why? Book*, "The point for us today is that we ought not to confuse the narrow and rigid and insensitive version of the Catholic tradition with the tradition itself." If Catholicism is not made as challenging and involving as other activities in life, today's youth will surely "tune out".

Even though much can be said for the liberalization of Catholic religious education, I worry about the notable absence of the richer parts of our past. Religious instruction is now viewed not so much as an intellectual undertaking, but as a social exercise—which in itself is closer to the early Christian ideals than to the orthodoxy of Roman Catholicism. I feel Catholic students today should know of the struggles that accompanied the Church's changes through the centuries, of the reformations that went before (including the most recent in the 1960s). To be Catholic should be to understand the nature of Catholicity, of Roman Catholicism with its Latin base and its complex history. Students should know the old rituals as well as the new; they should also be given the opportunity to master Latin and to be introduced to the wealth of liturgical music. They should know about the musicians, artists, writers, and scholars who added so much to the development of the European Church, and later the Church of the new world.

All these elements contribute to a Catholic's sense of belonging. It is imperative that the old way not be totally discarded in favour of modernism. One eighteen-year-old student I know, who has just joined a church choir, told me when we spoke of polyphony, and the works of Palestrina, "You know, I just can't believe what I've been missing."

In a report on Catholic high schools in his archdiocese during the year 1984–1985, Bishop (now Archbishop) Ambrozic of Toronto wrote that he feared that teachers, in an effort to make religion as attractive as possible, might "give the impression that Jesus is being offered to the students at the price which they are willing to pay." Jesus was the God most of the students he studied identified with; He was described by one as being the "nice guy" who would never permit anyone to go to Hell. The bishop reported too that there was a poorly developed sense of the "absoluteness of God's revelation and command, and of the Church's authority", the latter being to me a welcome element! But surely a balance should exist.

Just as the old ways of pre–Vatican II schooling fade in our memories, there has been a noticeable decline in Catholic school attendance. In 1964 there were 5.6 million children in the USA attending Catholic schools exclusively, from elementary to secondary school level; in 1986 the *New York Times* reported that the figure had decreased to 2.7 million. This sharp drop is attributed not so much to Catholic parents' wish for less restrictive religious upbringing for their children, as to the reality of the economic times—the Church can no longer afford to offer such exclusive private Catholic education any more. Instead, extracurricular activities are available to those who attend interdenominational schools—such as Sunday school, similar to the one I visited, for the elementary level, and retreat weekends for older children.

I believe the Church has a responsibility to reach out to youth—and to adults as well—to provide clubs where they can socialize, programs in which they can stretch their minds on theological and moral issues, and charities and social services in which they can contribute their Christian impulses to good effect.

I also think the Church has to work harder at bringing the lay and the clergy together on a friendly basis, so that each side can understand the other better. I have come across some parishes that are now doing this through discussion courses, held in an informal atmosphere. This openness and communication can only be a benefit to both sides.

A more difficult obstacle between the Church and the next generation is the rigidity the Church still maintains on issues like birth control, homosexuality, and women's liberation. I asked Father Donovan whether he thought many students would be alienated, as they grew older, by the Church's unyielding stand.

"You know," he said, "my guess is that, slowly and painfully, with some sidestepping at times, Catholicism will go more liberal. What we regarded as traditional will not disappear entirely but it will become less dominant. The right-wing elements in the Church are genuinely concerned about maintaining the old traditions, but I would say that they are stimulated largely by fear of the unknown—of change. I would call it partly a lack of trust in the workings of the Holy Spirit. We prefer to say 'Don't change anything—stay with the pattern laid down by the Apostles.' For one thing, most human beings tend to be conservative—but remember, that pattern didn't always work that well in the past either. Times change, people eventually change, society changes—and the pattern must change to accommodate new needs. That attitude is part of a world-wide phenomenon—the world is much changed outside the Catholic Church too. We don't know where we are going. I don't say that in a despairing or critical sense at all—it is exciting—but we are acknowledging that we do not have, we are not given, a clear indication of the route we have to take.

"I think that discovery is probably the most important, and probably the least successful, element in the Church's teaching today. I believe that Christianity is an adult religion. We do a lot—or the best we can—with children, but I think we have to look for ways to continue the education of Catholics—of Christians—beyond the school years. For most people, the last formal religious instruction is in the last class they attended in secondary school. In the Western world, the majority go on to university and don't do anything that has anything to do with religious education. The largest part of the human race doesn't go to university, and equally gets nothing. We have to come up with some way of convincing people of the significance of knowing more about their faith, at an adult level."

"Is there any clear way, though?" I asked. "Without the Church reverting to its old absolutist stance, which it clearly cannot do any more?"

"Of course, if we have faith," said Father Donovan, "we know, ultimately, that God is looking after us. But as far as showing the way is concerned, He is leaving an awful lot to us."

His words reminded me of a priest friend who once told me, "The Lord speaks to us quite clearly, you know. But we are very clever at not hearing him."

# 13

# WORLD WITHOUT END

"The real utopia is a world not to see but to see by."

— NORTHROP FRYE

We all understand that living life is in itself an education. But it was my father who once, at the breakfast table, when I realized I could no longer stomach bran cereal, put it all in perspective: "You finally discover, in your senior years," he said, "how many hours of sleep you really need, what sort of food and what sort of quantities of it you can stomach, whether it's better to run or walk to the train station, what kind of people you want to be around—and then you're dead!"

If it takes most of our life to educate ourselves about living, how can we ever find the time to get to know about our own death?

Since no one else who has died has come back to advise us all, we, as Christians, have to rely on Christ's experience. But the difficulty lies in interpreting His crucifixion, His resurrection, and His ascension as they relate to ourselves. We are left to find the way through further study, much conversation with others, and some serious thinking for ourselves.

This is obviously a topic of great complexity, and it would take a book in itself to do it justice. But a few points are worth setting out here, for further thought.

I'll begin at the beginning—with the Creed. American writer Michael Novak wrote in *Confession of a Catholic*, "Even

231

in our disagreements, it is the Creed that propels us." The Creed
is important to Catholics because it is the central reference for
interpretation of dogma and the basics of the faith, much more
so than the Psalms or the parables, or quotes from the prophets.
It also stands as a clear and clever piece of writing—a summary
of the complexities of Christ's message.

Consider the popular translation of the Nicene Creed:

We believe in one God, the Father, the almighty,
maker of heaven and earth, of all that is seen and unseen.
We believe in one Lord, Jesus Christ,
the only Son of God, eternally begotten of the Father,
God from God, Light from Light, true God from true God,
begotten, not made, one in Being with the Father.
Through him all things were made.
For us men and for our salvation he came down from heaven:
by the power of the Holy Spirit
he was born of the Virgin Mary, and became man.
For our sake he was crucified under Pontius Pilate;
he suffered, died, and was buried.
On the third day he rose again in fulfillment of the Scriptures;
he ascended into heaven
and is seated at the right hand of the Father.
He will come again in glory to judge the living and the dead,
and his kingdom will have no end.
We believe in the Holy Spirit, the Lord, the giver of life,
who proceeds from the Father and the Son.
With the Father and the Son he is worshipped and glorified.
He has spoken through the Prophets.
We believe in one holy catholic and apostolic Church.
We acknowledge one baptism for the forgiveness of sins.
We look for the resurrection of the dead,
and the life of the world to come. Amen.

It is interesting to ask ourselves how many times we have recited this, in our childhood and as adults, without thinking about the words. I know that when I stand to recite it in church on Sundays, I listen to the murmuring around me, the rise and fall of the voices. For instance, everyone chirps up happily for the first few lines, "We believe...," but many trail off when we come to "We believe in one holy catholic and apostolic Church...." I sometimes wonder whether this reticence is caused by lapse of memory or the fear of hypocrisy. I know many Catholics who have a problem believing in the Virgin birth, a communion of saints, even perhaps the resurrection of the dead; but one needs to read between the lines, so to speak, to understand that all sorts of hidden meanings are offered, that there is an advanced symbolic significance to the words of the Creed. We can find clues to these meanings in Christ's actions during His life. He made simple the complicated and unanswerable, as far as He was humanly able. He lived His life symbolically. Perhaps, if we view our own lives in a symbolic way, they may take on some order, manner, and meaning.

We are used, as Catholics, to responding to religious symbols, the most evident being the cross and the Trinity. Collectively they relate closely to the makeup of the human body—though there are contradictions here, as in the Church itself. The opposites—life and death, light and darkness, good and evil—are always there together, pulling one way and the other, working sometimes independently, sometimes together. A cross is a diagram of the body. The outstretched arms symbolize vulnerability, having no fear, offering and exposing oneself, but at the same time they symbolize bondage—pain, suffering, humiliation, and frustration.

With the sign of the cross we remind ourselves of our physical completeness and unity with God. By touching our foreheads we acknowledge God, the Father, with our heads and our minds; we point to our chests, our hearts, for the Son, Jesus

Christ, and our left and right shoulders for the Holy Spirit. The Trinity as a whole, made up of the rational and the irrational, the practical and the spiritual: the Father, who has laid down the theory, the law; the Son, who has shown, through living it, how it can be practised; and the Spirit, whose duty it is to guide our consciences and lead us towards enlightenment and truth during our lives and at the end of them.

The only way I can comprehend death and the afterlife is to see death itself as part of life. This is a phrase we've all heard a million times, I know, but the question that has engrossed me for a long time is, what does it really mean? Earlier in this book, Brian was quoted as viewing sin as "little deaths" in himself, which were followed by remorse, understanding, realization, and recovery. The whole notion of recovery and hope following the process of destruction is clear in the lines of the Creed "he suffered, died, and was buried" and "he rose again". Our spiritual bodies are destroyed, but—like the temple Christ referred to— they are raised again. Living symbolically, viewing our own lives as symbols, is an education in self-discovery.

The cross itself is a simple yet powerful symbol which stands for a number of Christian functions together. The most obvious is death, but it also stands for the hardships of life— loneliness, torture, pain, disgrace, abuse, sickness, separation, grief—life as a state of permanent Purgatory, suspended in limbo, stretched in suffering, humiliation. Christ referred to the cross well before the crucifixion.

> If any man would come after me, let him deny himself and take up his cross and follow me. For whoever would save his life will lose it; and whoever loses his life for my sake and the gospel's will save it.
>
> Mark 8:34–35

Perhaps misunderstanding the meaning of the cross is where many Catholics went wrong early in their lives. I know that I and many of my friends hung onto the suffering parts, and ignored the fact that it also could represent hope, truth, and light—the joyous aspects, the relief and renewal. We believed that relief would come to us only in the next life. In the meantime we'd have to sacrifice ourselves in this one, since we could only expect our reward after our spirits had risen leaving our rotten old bodies behind.

But however much thinking and analysing we may do, the thought of our own death never becomes any more comforting. We still fear it, and we have a right to do so, since it is incomprehensible to our three-dimensional minds in our three-dimensional world. I know that I fear prolonged pain—either physical or mental. I know I fear judgement—always, but more so, obviously, from the Supreme. I fear losing what is familiar, including who *I* am—my personality, my family and friends. I fear eternity, a state which never ends; I cannot comprehend a beginning and no end. But at the same time, I am fascinated: I can't wait! I have my own ideas of Heaven and I quite like the thought of being swallowed up to become part of another generation, a generation of spirits without all the miserable problems of worldly life and the barriers of humanity: shyness, different languages and customs, jealousy, envy, selfishness, and greed.... I quite like the association of ashes—that we were dust before and become dust again. It is comforting to consider, at times, that our life really is that meaning*less*. It can make it easier to deal with life's stresses.

If we attempt to view our lives as not necessarily our own, but just statistics in the big game plan, we find that we relinquish control over our own destiny, leaving it all to God. "Not my will be done" as Christ Himself put it while on the cross. Can this "giving in", this acknowledgement that one has no control over one's own destiny, make sense? Is it healthy? I believe giving in, spiritually, is the ultimate exercise in faith.

## On Earth As It Is in Heaven

> I think earth, if chosen instead of Heaven, will turn out to have been, all along, only a region in Hell: and earth, if put second to Heaven, to have been from the beginning a part of Heaven itself.
>
> C.S. Lewis, *The Great Divorce*

Christians are criticized constantly, and Catholics perhaps most of all, for maintaining that the next life will bring fulfilment only if we have suffered pain and grief in this one. I believe that the rewards we gain in this life—the happiness and joys we experience here—are just a sampling, a taste, of our own idea of Paradise. Our lives in this world are connected more closely with the next than we realize. This world *is* our "world without end", this life is both the rehearsal and the play. Novak describes it as "not a world whose end lies ever ahead; it is a world simultaneous."

If we have opportunities to glimpse pieces of our own Paradise here on earth, then of course we must be equipped to notice the Hell. Whatever Paradise means to each of us, it can only be evident as a feeling, since the original Paradise, the sinless society, fell centuries ago. But if we are to experience Paradise—to know what Heaven is all about—then Hell plays an important part in our lives.

Brian told me, "I do very strongly believe that the kingdom is here and now, and that I can praise God with all the world, as one with all God's creation. If I can be aware of that, I can be aware of what Heaven is about. Heaven is in my mind—not in my intellect but in my awareness as a human being. Sometimes, in certain states, I am aware that Heaven is here; and in certain cases Hell is here too and I put myself into Hell. Sometimes I think maybe there isn't anything else and I dissolve into God and don't have any awareness of myself as a separate being. Maybe that is what it is all about—I don't know. It is only in losing myself that I can gain myself, and that is something I am just discovering."

For Brian, this dissolving into God is a taste of the eventual absorption of the body into the soul, the last part of life's journey. Is it possible for our faith to follow a clearer path, our spiritual life to have more meaning, as the body ages towards decay? It was Carl Jung who compared the passage of life with the movement of the sun, from its rising in the east to its setting in the west. He suggested that in seeing our own ideals and behaviour as being "eternally valid", and being inclined to "make a virtue of unchangeably clinging to them," "we overlook the essential fact that the social goal is attained only at the cost of a diminution of personality."

But does this mean that, during this maturation, we lose our own identity? And how can this affect our souls? Will we be exposed to the ultimate fear—of not knowing who we are, and therefore losing sight of the purpose of our existence? Paul Tillich, in his book *The Courage to Be*, confronts those anxieties which accompany most of us through the ageing process.

> The anxiety of meaninglessness is anxiety about the loss of an ultimate concern, of a meaning which gives meaning to all meanings. This anxiety is aroused by the loss of a spiritual centre, of an answer, however symbolic and indirect, to the question of the meaning of existence.

Christ's resurrection offers us an answer. The appearance of the risen body of Christ, and His conversations after His death with the group of Apostles, illustrate that He was the same person as before. Does this indicate to us that the change from mortality to immortality does not really include the shedding of old skin?

While I am partial to the idea of becoming dust, John A. Hardon argues in his book *The Catholic Catechism* that the body becomes

> a spiritualized body; but it does not lose its corporeity. It remains truly human, though with an immortality coming from the divine strength, which enables the soul to so dominate the body that corruption can no longer enter what had formerly been subject to decay.

There are those who believe that death releases them from life. We often hear of So-and-so who died the way she lived—a sad, unhappy person—or those who die by their own hands, tormented souls who leave this life they have seen as a hell. But does committing suicide release one from oneself, when one's life is not naturally over, when God has not yet made the decision?

This question leads us to those very Catholic places known as Purgatory and Limbo. We were taught that Purgatory exists for preparation—for the journey heavenward—and is where atonement will be made for one's sins, while Limbo was a friendly substitute for Heaven where unbaptized babies could stay. Purgatory is and always has been part of our Catholic tradition. As children, we avidly collected "indulgences" (formal remissions which God would bestow on the departed souls in Purgatory) which would lessen their waiting time. Any questions on the existence of Purgatory itself could be explained by Christ's descent to the dead. Would He have gone to Hell? Is Purgatory an area of Hell, or of Heaven? But if He still assumed human form in His resurrected body, is there another message here—perhaps an even more obvious one? That we do our time in Purgatory on earth before we die?

In *On Death and Dying*, Elisabeth Kübler-Ross examined cases of people who were sick and close to death. She wrote, "The belief has long died that suffering here on earth will be rewarded in heaven. Suffering has lost its meaning." It is true that, in this day of advanced medical practice, we hope to escape physical pain. But many people do suffer spiritual torment, and experience "the dark night of the soul". Christ's experiences show us that it is possible for us to be participants in pain not only for ourselves but on behalf of others; through suffering we gain knowledge of ourselves, and through knowledge redemption. As Milan Kundera wrote in his novel *The Unbearable Lightness of Being*, "The heavier the burden, the closer our lives come to the earth, the more real and truthful they become."

I have spent time with people who knew they were dying, and I have observed enormous courage. I knew a woman who had been confined to a hospital bed, flat on her back, for five years, having lived longer than anyone expected, who made every patient in her ward laugh, and whose good spirits seemed virtually unnatural. Surely this was her Purgatory? What was there for her to be cheerful about? And I remember the day when Granny started her preparations to move out of our family home, where she had lived for over thirty years. She was in her late eighties, and had told me only a year previously that she was ready for death and would like to get on with it. She was a proud woman, but the courage she showed in giving up the things that were so familiar—the security of her home and family—at such an advanced age, to move into an old people's convent home, was, even to us, disturbing. She died one year later—of old age, in bed—and although her spirit is still very much around the house, and in our lives, I finally understood why she'd left home earlier. Like the woman in the hospital, she was preparing herself for another life. She knew how hard it would be for all of us if she died in the house.

My close friend Barbara flew back to England to be with her dying father. "It was an intellectual as well as an emotional experience," she told me. "In one week, he went from being abusive to all of us, being in pain and on all sorts of drugs, to being calm and peaceful. When I witnessed this upset and frustration in the earlier part of the week, I asked him what was happening, and he told me that he was not yet at the end, and therefore could not be at the beginning, but that he was going through the beginning of the end. It felt as though he were in a sort of limbo. He had nightmares, he wandered out of bed in the night, he was in despair yet angry about having us around. And then he gave in to the final destiny."

There is a famous book called *Life after Life*, by Raymond A. Moody, Jr., which recounts what happened to people who had "died" temporarily, for a few seconds or minutes. Some spoke of travelling and looking back on themselves—seeing their bodies as shells. A lot spoke of a feeling of weightlessness as they left their bodies, a lightness, a shedding of the former heaviness of self—the ascension, perhaps, the new spiritual body taking shape. Most found it difficult to put into words exactly what they had experienced. One woman suggested that the world she entered, or was about to enter, was not something she could describe within the restrictions of mortal language. Many people mentioned the feeling of "peace, quiet, and comfort"—a beauty and a relief, no pain, just relaxation. Some heard majestic and beautiful music. Nearly all spoke of "the being of light", the love and warmth which were evident. One said that the light was of "perfect understanding and perfect love". Another mentioned that when she was leaving her body she felt the aid of "spiritual helpers", which perhaps might make sense of the idea of guardian angels (finally!) Some mentioned their feelings of "coming home".

I find the travelling aspect the most intriguing—many of those interviewed referred to journeying along dark tunnels, which one person described as an airless cylinder which gave him a "feeling of limbo, of being half-way there, and half-way somewhere else." Finally they came to the warm light of love, and it was there that they were judged. But it was not what they had expected. This "review", as one person termed it, took the form of "probing, non-verbal questions" about her life, or significant parts of it, which were flashed before her. They spoke of the simple message communicated to them during the review—that the two most important things in life are learning to love other people and the pursuit of knowledge.

When these people recovered, of course, their lives had taken on new meaning. A number had had no religious affiliation at all and turned to Christianity. They changed in the way they viewed others and others' needs. They said their experiences had "made life much more precious."

These accounts, if one believes them, are exceptional. What a luxury it would be if we could all physically die for a minute, see the light, and return to make amends! But this would be too easy: Christ said, "Blessed are those who have not seen and yet believe." (John 20:29) One lesson we can take away, perhaps, is that the Day of Judgement, the "review", is not necessarily an event we should expect only at the end of our lives, but something we can, through prayer and the examination of our consciences, experience regularly during our lives. This is the real meaning of the expression "Life is a trial." C.S. Lewis wrote in *A Grief Observed*:

> In this trial [God] makes us occupy the dock, the witness box, and the bench all at once. He always knew that my temple was a house of cards. His only way of making me realize the fact was to knock it down.

As Christians, we believe that there is light at the end of the tunnel, in life and after life. We know the ups and downs. We know that only after descent can ascension follow. I remember a conversation I had with an elderly Catholic man who had been sick for a long time. We were talking about the necessity of hope, of a belief in the future, the unknown. He said, "If you can't see it, it is hard to know why you are here at all. Seeing the light and losing the light and looking at it again is what it's all about. You can't appreciate the light without the light, and in the darkness we have to look to the light. We can't just sit in the dark."

Light, of course, is the symbol of enlightenment and hope. Christ said, "I am the way, the truth and the Light." The Old Testament records that messages from God were given in light visions and dreams. Paul, blinded by light on the road to Damascus, was enlightened thereafter. "I am the light of the world," Jesus said; "He who follows me will not walk in darkness, but will have the light of life." (John 8:12)

Brian told me of an experience he had in his sleep: "I had a dream recently where I was on top of a mountain after climbing up it with difficulty, and there were two men up there who appeared from nowhere, each carrying a briefcase, a small attaché case. I felt very scared. The men were dressed in black and my fear was because I knew that this attaché case contained all the written records of my sins. I asked 'Who are you?' They didn't say anything, and I said then, 'What have you got in the briefcase?' and they opened it and out came my soul. And my soul was beautiful—the colour of gold in aura—and I just couldn't believe it! It was a great surprise to me, it wasn't at all what I thought my soul would look like, and it was wonderful. I realized too that it was feminine—not a masculine thing at all—no jagged edges. As I went over to look more closely, I noticed that one of the men was myself and the other one was either God or God's messenger. This was my revelation of completeness—of becoming wholly yourself."

What Brian's dream signified to me was that our souls probably have all the clues. Carrying our personalities, and our baggage of sins and physical torments, finally, at the end of our lives, they are released like a bird from a cage. It was Plato who referred to the soul as a prisoner in the body. The release is the immortal emerging from the mortal, a cutting of the umbilical cord of humanity, a flight from the old sin-infested body towards a freedom of the spirit. The idea of our souls heading towards a destination of warmth and light to meet their Maker makes impending death rather comforting. How wonderful to shed all the old restrictions and sufferings of human life, to enter a perfect world!

This relinquishment may be what Paul was referring to when he said, "For our knowledge is imperfect and our prophecy is imperfect; but when the perfect comes, the imperfect will pass away." (I Corinthians 13:9)

## As It Was in the Beginning, Is Now and Ever Shall Be

I believe that the answers to our questions on the meaning of life and our eventual release from it lie with the Holy Spirit, the most mysterious partner of the Trinity. It is only a few of the older Catholics I've spoken to who openly admit to praying and communicating with the "ghost" of God. Apart from the image of the bird—the dove of peace portrayed in so many great paintings—the Holy Spirit is commonly viewed as the symbol of truth, enlightenment, and freedom in perfect formlessness. Perhaps this lack of form makes it difficult for us to comprehend the Holy Spirit, because it seems to me it represents not only the mortal but the immortal too.

So how are we to understand, how do we learn to communicate fully and confidently with a formless deity, preparing ourselves for the next life, for the everlasting happiness to come? Is the way to obey Church law, honour the messages of papal documents, regularly attend Mass, receive the Sacraments, do Christian deeds, examine our consciences, communicate with God the Father, the Son, and the Holy Spirit, ask questions, read the scriptures, and believe in humanity, in the service of the community, in love? To abide by all of these, or just a few? All of the time or just part of it? Fully, or half-heartedly? Are the clues to the truth to be found in the practice of Roman Catholicism or in the words of Christ, or both?

For each of us, the answer may be different. But as Catholics we do have a duty: C.S. Lewis wrote that "happiness, as you will come to see when you are older, lies in the path of duty." Milan Kundera wrote, "happiness is the longing for repetition." But happiness, whatever makes us happy, seems shortlived if God is not a part of it. If, as we were taught as young Catholics—perhaps badly—God has a place in our lives, then it is our responsibility to define that place and make room for Him. We've been given some directions in prayer and scripture to the ways of hearing His voice, but I believe that only through self-education, by question and answer, will the truth emerge. Only then, perhaps, will the imprisonment of our mortal life seem bearable.

I asked myself, as I was travelling along through this book, and reaching the end of this particular spiritual journey, how I was to end. I knew it would be presumptuous of me to attempt to offer a neat summary of solutions to all Catholics' religious concerns. This was never my intention. But I do hope I may have helped a few of my fellow Catholics by probing my own conscience and retelling moments in my own life and the lives of others which I felt were significant. Instead I will leave the final word to a man who has written so simply and so well about the complexity of Christianity. I quote the following from *The Great Divorce* as a tribute to the genius of C.S. Lewis:

Time is the very lens through which ye see—small and clear, as men see through the wrong end of a telescope—something that would otherwise be too big for ye to see at all. That thing is Freedom: the gift whereby ye most resemble your Maker and are

244

yourselves parts of eternal reality. But ye can see it only through the lens of Time, in a little clear picture, through the inverted telescope. It is a picture of moments following one another and yourself in each moment making some choice that might have been otherwise. Neither the temporal succession nor the phantom of what ye might have chosen and didn't is itself Freedom. They are a lens. The picture is a symbol: but it's truer than any philosophical theorem (or, perhaps, than any mystic's vision) that claims to go behind it. For every attempt to see the shape of eternity except through the lens of Time destroys your knowledge of Freedom. Witness the doctrine of Predestination which shows (truly enough) that eternal reality is not waiting for a future in which to be real; but at the price of removing Freedom which is the deeper truth of the two. And wouldn't Universalism do the same? Ye *cannot* know eternal reality by a definition. Time itself, and all acts and events that fill Time, are the definition, and it must be lived. The Lord said we were gods. How long could ye bear to look (without Time's lens) on the greatness of your own soul and the eternal reality of her choice?

# ACKNOWLEDGEMENTS

Biblical quotations are from *The Holy Bible: Revised Standard Version: An Ecumenical Edition* (Common Bible), copyright © 1973 by the Division of Christian Education of the National Council of the Churches of Christ in the United States of America. Used by kind permission.

Excerpts from *The Catholic Catechism* copyright © 1975 by John A. Hardon. Used by kind permission of Doubleday & Company Inc., New York.

Excerpts from *The Great Divorce* copyright © 1946 by C.S. Lewis.

Excerpts from *The Code of Canon Law*, English translation, copyright © 1983 The Canon Law Society Trust.

# BIBLIOGRAPHY

Saint Augustine. *Confessions*. Translated by R.S. Pine-Coffin.1961. Reprint. Harmondsworth, England: Penguin Books, 1981.

Bettelheim, Bruno. *The Uses of Enchantment: The Meaning and Importance of Fairy Tales*. New York: Random House, Vintage Books, 1977.

Block, Walter; Brennan, Geoffrey; and Elzinga, Kenneth; eds. *Morality of the Market: Religious and Economic Perspectives*. Vancouver: The Fraser Institute, 1985.

Bokenkotter, Thomas. *Essential Catholicism*. Garden City: Doubleday, 1985.

Bryant, Christopher. *Jung and the Christian Way*. Minneapolis: The Seabury Press, 1983.

Canon Law Society of Great Britain and Ireland. *The Code of Canon Law*. London: Collins Liturgical Publications, 1983.

Gilligan, Carol. *In a Different Voice: Psychological Theory and Women's Development*. Cambridge, Massachusetts: Harvard University Press, 1982.

Greeley, Andrew M. *The Catholic WHY? Book*. Chicago: The Thomas More Press, 1983.

Hardon, John A. *The Catholic Catechism*. Garden City: Doubleday, 1975.

Johnson, Edwin Clark. *In Search of God in the Sexual Underworld*. New York: Quill, 1983.

Joyce, James. *A Portrait of the Artist as a Young Man*. 1916. Reprint. New York: Penguin Books, 1983.

Kübler-Ross, Elisabeth. *On Death and Dying*. New York: Macmillan, 1969.

Kundera, Milan. *The Unbearable Lightness of Being*. Translated by Michael Henry Heim. 1984. Reprint. London: Faber & Faber, 1985.

Küng, Hans. *What Must Remain in the Church*. Translated by Edward Quinn. Glasgow: Collins, Fontana, 1977.

Lewis, C.S. *The Great Divorce: A Dream*. 1946. Reprint. Glasgow: Collins, Fount Paperbacks, 1983.

——. *A Grief Observed*. 1961. Reprint. London: Faber & Faber, 1978.

——. *The Problem of Pain*. 1940. Reprint. Glasgow: Collins, 1978.

Mall, David. *In Good Conscience: Abortion and Moral Necessity*. Libertyville, Illinois: Kairos Books, 1982.

Moody, Raymond A., Jr. *Life after Life*. Reprint. 1975. New York: Bantam, 1976.

Novak, Michael. *Confession of a Catholic*. San Francisco: Harper & Row, 1983.

Payer, Pierre J. *Sex and the Penitentials: The Development of a Sexual Code 550–1150*. Toronto: University of Toronto Press, 1984.

Peters, Thomas J., and Waterman, Robert H., Jr. *In Search of Excellence*. 1982. Reprint. New York: Warner Books, 1984.

Priestland, Gerald. *Priestland's Progress: One Man's Search for Christianity Now*. London: British Broadcasting Corporation, 1981.

Progoff, Ira, trans. *The Cloud of Unknowing*. 1957. Reprint. New York: Dell, Laurel, 1983.

Read, Piers Paul. Quoted in *Why I Am Still a Catholic*, Robert Nowell, ed. Collins.

Schaeffer, Susan Fromberg. *The Madness of a Seduced Woman*. London: Hamish Hamilton, 1984.

Teilhard de Chardin, Pierre. *On Happiness*. Translated by René Hague. London: Collins, 1973.

Thomas, Lewis. *The Lives of a Cell: Notes of a Biology Watcher*. 1974. Reprint. New York: Bantam, 1983.

Tillich, Paul. *The Courage to Be*. New Haven, Connecticut: Yale University Press, 1952.

Weaver, Mary Jo. *New Catholic Women: A Contemporary Challenge to Traditional Religious Authority*. San Francisco: Harper & Row, 1985.

Yallop, David. *In God's Name*. London: Jonathan Cape, 1984.

*PUBLICATIONS OF THE HOLY SEE*

*Gaudium et Spes: Pastoral Constitution on the Church in the Modern World*. Promulgated by Pope Paul VI. Boston: Daughters of St. Paul, 1965.

*Instruction on Respect for Human Life in Its Origin and on the Dignity of Procreation*. Vatican translation. Sherbrooke, Quebec: Editions Paulines, 1987.

*Of Human Life* (Humanae Vitae), Pope Paul VI. Translated by the NC News Service. Boston: Daughters of St. Paul, 1968.

*Prayers and Devotions from Pope John XXIII*, ed. Rev. John P. Donnelly. Translated by Dorothy White. London: Burns & Oates, 1967.